Praise for
I Never Heard You Cry
A Compassionate Journey Through Abortion

"*I Never Heard You Cry* . . . never approaches political edict or social commentary regarding abortion. Ardyce West focuses rather on the substantial number of people who do struggle with complex and deeply emotional post-abortion issues."
- *Publisher*

"For me, a great book is one that leaves me moved and tingling when I complete its final passages. Ardyce West's book, *'I Never Heard You Cry'*, did precisely that for me. Not only will you be supported and inspired, you will find numerous springs of healing in this book. It is poignant as well as practical, offering compassion and insight in a controversial and troubled arena. Read this book and let your heart be touched." - *Dr. Roger W. Teel, Senior Minister and Spiritual Director, Mile Hi Church, Lakewood, Colorado*

"Ardyce West courageously shares her vulnerability in exposing her soul's journey of healing after her experience of abortion. Her insights give us all strength in moving forward after irreplaceable loss into greater awareness. *'I Never Heard You Cry'* is a significant and much needed work that will heal lives." - *Rev. Christian Sorensen, D.D., Seaside Center for Spiritual Living, Encinitas, CA*

"This extraordinary book isn't about pro-life, pro-choice, politics or religion. It's about people - the vast majority of us who understand that abortion is not a black-and-white issue that can only be addressed in absolutes. While it is an essential book for those who are struggling with unexpected and unattended post-abortion grief, it's also an excellent book for parents to share with their kids to help them learn about consequences and accountability." - *Kevin Cahill, Author, Sand Creek, Letters to a Rose, The Last Cafe, Knights of Harvest*

What reviewers are saying on Amazon.com:

"Few know how to heal the emotional wounds that accompany abortion. We don't talk about it much. This book is a good place to begin. It speaks with compassion, and offers signposts to acceptance, forgiveness, and healing." - *T. Nash*

"This book attempts to sort it out without all the screaming, finger-pointing and useless drama. I applaud this author for bringing some peace to all the pain on both sides of this serious and divisive issue." - *Jane*

"It has been written with such care and compassion while elevating us beyond the false oversimplification of this being a matter merely of either pro-life or pro-choice." - *Bruce*

"It was like finding Spring water in the desert of judgment that surrounds abortion and other such life decisions that many face in this complicated world." - *Suzanne*

"This book should be given to anyone considering or has been through an abortion." - *Susan*

"The book is about so much more than the journey through abortion, it speaks to me on many different levels about my own experiences in life." - *Frannie*

"I would highly recommend *"I Never Heard You Cry"* for anyone facing a healing process or anyone who works in an area of healing or spiritual counseling." - *Carol*

E-book also available on Kindle and other devices

Ardyce West is a Spiritual Counselor and a licensed Life Mastery Consultant and DreamBuilder Coach. She assists others in living a wholehearted life by providing guidance and life coaching for individuals and groups. She has led various art workshops and chaired large retreats for multi-faceted healing conferences. Also an accomplished artist, she lives in Colorado with her husband.

I Never Heard You Cry

I Never Heard You Cry

A Compassionate Journey Through Abortion

Ardyce West

LoneWolf

Paperback first published April 2016 by KC LoneWolf
admin@kclonewolf.com
Littleton, CO

ISBN-10: 0996954414
ISBN-13: 978-0-9969544-1-9

E-book edition also available on Kindle and other devices
E-book first published electronically 2011 by KC LoneWolf
admin@kclonewolf.com
Littleton, CO

Author contact information: admin@ardyce.org

Printed in the United States of America

For all the children who were not allowed to enter into this world. I write this with love on behalf of their sacrifice. I specifically dedicate this to Lanie, my guide and my angel. She continues to teach me compassion, gentleness, and great love.

Contents

Foreword

There are topics that ignite courageous conversations and create controversy. The subject matter of this book is one of those topics. Abortion has been and continues to be a "hot bed" of heated discussion in numerous circles. There are groups of people with opinions that connect the choice to have an abortion to morality. Other groups are adamant that a woman has the right to choose what happens with her body. Still others are fighting for the rights for abortion for medical safety of the woman.

According to statistics, nearly half of the pregnancies among American women are unintended, and four in 10 of these are terminated by abortion. Twenty-two percent of all pregnancies (excluding miscarriages) end in abortion. From 1973 through 2008, nearly 50 million legal abortions occurred. Each year, two percent of women aged 15-44 have an abortion and half have had at least one previous abortion.

Ardyce West has written a deeply personal and important book with a message for anyone who has ever had an abortion or experienced a loved one having an abortion. She invites us to understand the long lasting emotional and psychological aftermath that comes from moving through an abortion. She also invites us to replace fear with love. Through her personal story and others sharing their stories, Ardyce invites us to move into a state of compassionate listening and profound forgiveness. In fact, she asks us to move out of any form of judgment and open our hearts to anyone who has ever had to experience the pain of abortion on any level.

I have known Ardyce for many years and her commitment to sharing this important message has been unwavering. I have witnessed her deep dedication to supporting people in being healthy and whole. That commitment and her personal work make this a powerful tool. This is a book that will support healing and transform the way people look at abortion if they are willing to suspend fearful concepts. I highly encourage you to read this book and share it with your family, friends, and even counseling clients. It will make a difference in how they view the experience of abortion and hopefully encourage them to open their hearts.

Cynthia James
Author
What Will Set You Free
Revealing Your Extraordinary Essence
You Are Loved
www.cynthiajames.net

Author Notes

I am often asked the origin and meaning of my name. In my late twenties, I was working one day at my job as Head Concierge of one of Denver's finest hotels. It was a high-energy day, like most during the busy noon hour. The elegant century-old hotel lobby was bathed by brilliant sunlight shining through the multi-colored stained glass skylight overhead.

Above the din I heard a question addressed to me in a Scottish brogue, "Do ya know what your name means, lassie?"

I turned and noticed a handsome young man about my age, with dark curly hair and a spark in his blue eyes. He had read my nametag - Ardyce. I smiled and replied, "I've been told that it is French."

"Actually, because of the way it is spelled, it's Scottish," he said. "The 'dyce' part of your name is a nautical term, meaning, 'to hold her close - to hold the sail close to the ship so it goes in the right direction.'"

Surprised, I replied, "Well, I guess my parents named me correctly. I try to go in the right direction..."

This simple encounter created a curiosity in me, for he seemed to appear out of nowhere and then disappear just as quickly. I checked the hotel roster for his name. He was not registered as a guest. This two-minute interaction created a quantum shift in my life's direction.

Throughout our lives, many people show up as

guides, creating opportunities for change. What he said made me question if my sail indeed was "close to the ship." I began to wonder if I *was* going in the right direction. My life was not going the way I intended. I was in a relationship that wasn't working. I no longer wanted to be involved with someone who was caught up in the addictive patterns of drug and alcohol abuse. And, although I loved my job, I made very little money and wanted to do something more meaningfully related to my artistic gifts. Indeed, my sail was just flopping in the breeze. I was barely treading water and certainly going nowhere. I concluded it was time to set my sail for a true destination, but the direction I had traveled for some time had momentum of its own, which delayed my newly intended voyage. The storms that followed changed the course of my life.

This is the account of my voyage through some rough seas and how I have learned to navigate in alignment with the Zenith, the divine source of my being that I call Spirit, God, the Divine, which helps me stay the course. I am now intentionally heading toward destinations of deep meaning and heart after taking stock of the passages that led me to this point. This is but a portion of my journey - of what it means for me to hold the sail close so my ship sails in the right direction.

Introduction

This book is intended to help heal the hearts of women and men who have experienced the pain of abortion. It is written to acknowledge our grief, which we so often deny and try to repress due to narrow-minded societal and religious condemnation. By recognizing that we share many common experiences, together we can work through our challenges and strive to heal on a heart-level through understanding and compassion, thus honoring our journey through the passages of life.

My own healing centers on the writing process which enables me to delve deep within and to work through the fears that hinder me from navigating my life's direction. I put pen to paper when nothing else seems to assuage my need to search. So, I write.

It is a spilling of the mind, a purging of thoughts. But eventually, what begins with a conglomeration of questions about what life means ends up in clarity of purpose. Daily meditation, deep study, and consistently asking questions into the Universal Field result in a mystical awareness of unexpected answers that open me to greater dimensions of conscious awareness. For light to shine into the dark abyss, we must be open to such awareness. We must be willing to change.

One of the major issues in my life that I finally faced was the secret I had harbored about my abortion. I am an external processor. I must speak out loud or write what is on my mind to achieve deeper understanding of the creative power working in my life. As I developed more confidence to reveal the truth about my wounded heart to my circle of trusted family and friends, I felt an enormous weight lifting off my shoulders. When I began to expand my comfort zone and discuss it with mild acquaintances or strangers, what happened more often than not would be a confession of their own complicity in something similar. It seemed to be such a relief for them to admit their own deep secret to someone else who understood what "we just don't talk about."

Unexpected tears would come to their eyes, because they, too, have been deeply affected by the decision to let go of their child. Some were not just stories of their own experience, but of their involvement with someone close who had to make such a decision. Both women and men were eager to share their experiences and tell me what they had learned, and how in some cases they overcame their personal struggles with shame, guilt, regret, and grief.

When it comes to abortion, we are reluctant to reveal the broken heart that often results. This is *the red-hot topic* that no one wants to broach in any circle. With similar soul experiences, however, we who have had abortions – both women *and* men - must silently grieve alone often in shame or fear of the many social, political, and religious stigmas attached.

There was a time when I viewed my life from my "small self," believing the hand I was dealt was the way it was, living a life of victimization. I believed I had no control over the outcome. I lived many years within the grasp of the past, hiding in uneasy solitude, safe and out of harm's way. I was responding to the effects of my fears, instead of making conscious choices that *affect* the cause. At times I compromised my ideals and principles by trying to fit into relationships and career choices that were not natural for me. As a result I remained small.

When I finally realized that we live in a world of cause and effect, life began to shift toward what I aspired to be, instead of living within repeated patterns of what I no longer desired. What I think about this moment is the cause. The actions I take based upon my thought, being the cause of my action, create the effects. This is the creative process of cause and effect.

Making conscious choices or thinking better thoughts generate improved actions, therefore creating more of what I want to occur. It is up to me. My choice of thought affects my choice of action, resulting in how life responds to what I am thinking. Contrarily, if I do not make healthy choices, what results are effects that I constantly have to clean up long after the results are in. For many years, this was my life. It was only by recognizing these repeated patterns did I begin to see that I was not in control and certainly not safe. If I wanted to change, I had to be more honest with myself, for I was the common denominator in all that was happening in my life.

I began to question why I was afraid to be my greatest self. What was I running from, and what was I afraid to remember? I took account of what was diminishing me. The source of the negative pattern was a fear of the past that I had not yet acknowledged. More questions began to arise. I had to stand in my truth by going back to what I chose to not remember, so I could heal and build a new foundation on which to stand. I needed a new voice from which to speak, and a wide-open heart to love myself and others. This was the genesis of my journey to self-forgiveness for my abortion and healing the wounds of my past.

What began, in this book, as an account of my journey to self-healing, has become a dedication to the many people who have suffered the pain, guilt, regret, and shame of abortion. At the request of those who generously agreed to share their stories, I have changed their names to protect their privacy, which illustrates the nature of the beast of the secrecy that shrouds this deeply personal subject. Here, I give voice to and honor the millions of people who suffer in silence. Most importantly, I give voice on behalf of the children we have left behind.

Chapter One

The Elephant in the Room

It is not my intention to support either the principles of the extreme left of pro-choice, or the extreme right of pro-life. These contentious opinions cannot be ignored, however. Their points of view meld politics, ethics, morality, and religion. I like to call it *poligion.*

Despite all the *poligious* wrangling, the vast majority of people with whom I discuss abortion take a moderate stance, believing in both the right to life, but also in a woman's right to choose abortion. Fanatics on the right call abortion murder; extremists on the left deny the unborn any right to life until the first breath is taken. Most of us in the middle compassionately understand that there are many individual and unique circumstances involved in a woman's – or teenager's -

life-altering decision to terminate a pregnancy. Unfortunately, the extremists are comfortable spreading false propaganda, threats of retaliation, and in some sadly disturbing cases, violence to make their point. Thanks to a media that feeds on sensational headlines, we are bombarded by coverage of these diametrically opposed opinions. One must dig deeper to access more thoughtful and levelheaded debate.

The pro-life movement supports primarily religious and political views, insisting that life begins at conception and ends at natural death. Therefore, an embryo and a fetus are considered to be "persons" with a legal and moral right to life. Many traditional religious organizations hold the same position. Abstention is the steadfast and unbending rule. Adoption is the only answer to unwanted pregnancy. Only in cases of health concerns for the life of the mother and for the fetus, or in cases of incest or rape, should abortion be allowed. Sometimes, even under these circumstances, not all cases are considered a good reason for abortion. Extreme fundamentalists go a step farther, opposing the use of contraceptives or any other means intended to prevent natural conception.

On the other hand, the pro-choice movement

supports political and ethical opinion that a woman has the implicit right to make her own healthcare decisions, which includes the right to continue or terminate her pregnancy. For women who choose to carry their pregnancies to term, pro-choice advocates support state or privately funded programs to assist the poor in raising the child or adoption placement. Pro-choicers actively support reproductive rights legislation, sexual education, and fertility treatments. Pro-choice advocates further argue that anti-abortion legislation, if ratified, is unconstitutional and would do nothing more than return us to the dark days of illicit and dangerous abortions.

Both pro-life and pro-choice positions are based on strong belief systems that, on paper, are backed by reasonable facts and arguments. Sadly, however, what we often see from both sides are misguided attempts to create fear and intimidation through violence meant to force their will on the opposition. Politicians are shouted down during election rallies, medical clinics are vandalized or sometimes in extreme cases burned or bombed, physicians have been assaulted and murdered, and young men and women are verbally attacked and taunted outside of clinics.

On her way to buy flowers in a neighborhood of shops and restaurants, a good friend of mine recently encountered a noisy anti-abortion picket line of about twenty people, primarily men and a just a few women. As she approached, she noticed they were loudly protesting in front of a family planning clinic. A young couple was violently confronted by the protesters as they attempted to walk into the building. The picketers blocked the entrance, making verbal threats and pushing the couple back with their signs - an act tantamount to emotional terrorism. The couple tearfully ran the gauntlet, ducking through the protestors, who were acting like a pack of ravenous wolves.

My friend said that, over the din, she heard someone cry, "For God's sake, where is the compassion?" She heard this over and over as she walked past the protesters, only to suddenly realize that it was she who was screaming at the crowd. She said she believed something arose from deep within her to speak on behalf of a greater consciousness. The protesters fell silent, apparently surprised that a single person had the courage to stand up to them. She said that she was so traumatized and concerned for the couple that she wandered for several blocks just to become grounded again, never buying her flowers after all.

Conversely, another dear friend of mine, who was a representative of a large conservative political organization, was the target of death threats from pro-choice supporters during a recent political campaign. He was forced to seek police protection for both him and his family until long after the election ended.

What we put our focus on creates more of the same. If we push against something and generate negative energy, we get more of what we do not want. When we push forward for something with positive energy, in support of its betterment, our experience infinitely expands. The extremist pro-abortion and anti-abortion advocates promote what is wrong with the opposing view, rather than thoughtfully defending their beliefs with compassion for those who are struggling with an unwanted, or unhealthy pregnancy. Negative action only generates negative reaction.

Poligious websites are plastered with propaganda, quoting politicians, religious leaders, and even celebrities. They include the inevitable supportive links and pleas for donations "to fight against" the opposition. Nowhere on these sites is a helping hand extended to those seeking guidance and intelligent information about pregnancy, abortion, and related health issues. There is no sensitivity, no compassion; only anger, hatred, and often lies. This vitriolic dialogue and negative propaganda simply panders to fear.

Many of us are familiar with the ancient story about the blind men and the elephant. Six blind men touch an elephant and describe what they see in their minds. An argument ensues because each man's perception is different. Since perception of truth is relative, what is true for one is not for another. Each viewpoint is accurate according to the individual's perspective, but when misunderstood and not objectively communicated, these varying views become points of dissention.

The topic of abortion is the elephant in the room. It is gigantic, it creates tremendous discomfort, and nobody wants to talk about it. No matter whose company we are in, if the topic of abortion enters the conversation you can almost feel the room tighten up. We tread lightly until we know just where we stand, dancing carefully in fear of offending someone or setting off an argument. What is more often than not communicated is left in the mystery. But, if we look at abortion as a human issue, not embroiled in politics and religion, we remove the veil, the defensive posture, and create an avenue for compassion and understanding. If we could share and discuss our opinions and experiences in a setting of reasonable cooperation, free of judgment and intimidation, some might discover what it is like to walk in another's shoes. For example, when my friend confronted the angry anti-abortion protesters, pleading for compassion, their sudden silence clearly indicated a shift from the mob mentality.

It's not unreasonable to conclude that we, as rational and compassionate beings, support the fundamental right to life. The matter of choice, however, is shrouded in a thousand shades of gray, despite what the poligious fringe wants to believe. Choice always relates to consequence. It is the law of cause and effect.

Because we are human, we possess the ability to make choices, to have volition, and to live as we intend. From those choices, consequences result. Thoughtful evaluation of the possible consequences prior to decision-making can lead us to a more conscious way of life. The result is a life lived on a higher level from the heart, directed by the wisdom within.

Let's take off the blinders, drop the boxing gloves and picket signs, and create meaningful dialogue about the elephant in the room. It takes courage to open our hearts to each other, specifically on the subject of abortion. We must stand for a higher truth.

Chapter Two

The Void

Everything I was taught to believe, I was now going against. "Thou shalt not kill" kept going through my mind. But what about me? I had been warned that carrying my child to term was a legitimate risk to my life. Was I not justified to put that into the mix of decision-making? And what about the baby's health? My doctor made it clear, should we both survive the birth, the probability of a healthy child was unlikely.

My best friend Clare drove me to the clinic. I anticipated arriving in front of a run-down building on a back lot hidden from view - a dark, foreboding atmosphere like something from an old B movie. I was surprised to find a contemporary office park, well groomed with beautiful landscaping of grass, flowers, and trees. The décor of the clinic was tasteful and soothing, the wall art a sea motif with shades of sandy-toned sea shells and pastel shades of teal, green, and peach.

The atmosphere helped me feel more comfortable until the office manager, who appeared to be on automatic pilot, handed me a clipboard with all necessary forms and disclaimers attached. Back to reality. I was overwhelmed, not knowing what to feel. There were so many emotions attached to the experience. Fear, pain, and anguish were precursors to the guilt and shame to follow.

After filling out the forms and signing my life off to the medical gods, the all too familiar waiting room vigil began. We sat, making small talk for about thirty minutes. It was an appropriate name, The Waiting Room. I had waited six agonizingly long weeks for this day, and this last hour was the longest. Nervous anticipation of the unknown is always far worse than the event itself. Time seemed to stand still. Little did I know that within an hour I would soon experience that very phenomenon of no time or space.

Before I was escorted to another room, I remember

telling Clare what I wanted her to do - just in case I didn't survive the procedure. She listened patiently, and then she looked at me with a depth of compassion and told me she'd be waiting to drive me home when it was over. Knowing I was supported helped me follow through with what I came there to do.

I then spoke with a counselor, who advised me to carefully consider my options. With great concern she encouraged me to make sure my decision was the right one, emphasizing that I could still change my mind. I didn't have to go through with this if I didn't want to. This was not what I wanted, but I had to do it. As far as considering my options, there had been little else on my mind. Based on all the information that I had gathered, I made the decision that was right for me. My mind was made up.

After confirming my pregnancy a few weeks before that day, I consulted my trusted family physician. I was looking for answers that were not there. I wanted him to tell me that it was all a mistake – that the tests were not positive. Instead, I got the news I didn't want to hear, and more. Even during that early stage of my pregnancy, my life was already threatened, as was the life of the child. He told me that, due to a rare disease I had, a pregnancy could not only bring extreme consequences for my long-term health and well-being, but it could possibly claim my life in the process. Also, because of medications I was taking, the baby's heart could be severely damaged. If she were to survive, she would likely face several heart surgeries from the time of her birth, and for many years to come.

He told me that the physical and emotional stress of the pregnancy and its complications could create even more health challenges. I would likely require hospitalization for at least six of the nine months, incurring hundreds of thousands of dollars in medical bills. Without adequate medical insurance, I was facing not only a health crisis for me and my child, but also a financial catastrophe in the event that one or both of us did survive.

My doctor advised it would be best if I didn't have children at all. Several years earlier, I suffered a miscarriage. As a young wife, just twenty years old, I was emotionally devastated. Not only had we lost our baby, but my mother was dying of cancer. I wanted her to know my baby, her grandchild, before she left. Ten months later she died. Because of that miscarriage, and in light of this difficult pregnancy, I finally understood that bearing children was not a part of this life's journey. I loved kids. I wanted to be a mother, but it appeared that I was not to be one. I was to do something else that had meaning.

There were numerous other complications. I was single and had no one to share the responsibility, for the birth father was not involved, by his choice and by my own. I had no financial means to support the circumstances of such an extreme medical challenge. What was I to do? One choice seemed to be the only obvious option. Abortion.

I had to do it, but this choice flew in the face of everything I was taught to believe. Shame and guilt consumed me - shame for behaving so recklessly in becoming pregnant by not taking proper precautions, and guilt for feeling like I was doing something wrong, even though I knew it was the best choice. To mitigate these seemingly inexcusable acts, I created a void within to protect myself from the emotional pain. I was very impatient to put this all behind me. The sooner I got this over with, the sooner I could move on - or so I thought.

Finally, I was taken into the surgical suite. Small treatment rooms encircled the main desk. I undressed in one of these rooms and then eased back on a cold table, wearing nothing but a hospital gown with paper sheets covering my legs. The overhead lights were off, shrouding the room in dismal shades of gray. I looked around at the medical equipment. By the head of the table was an oxygen tank with a mask hanging on it. A small rolling table sat at the foot of the examining table, loaded with medical instruments under a towel. Except for the faint glow of several monitors around me, the only other light in the room was a surgical lamp hanging from the ceiling at the end of the table. Within the walls of this small, sterile room I suddenly felt very tiny and insignificant. I was so frightened.

The doctor finally entered, accompanied by two nurses. In the same way that I was surprised by the atmosphere of the clinic, I was equally surprised by the handsome young man standing in front of me. I expected an old, slump-shouldered man with wild gray hair, speaking in a dialect I could hardly under-stand. I had in mind some mad scientist from an old 1950's horror film that I watched in the dark chill of the basement as a kid on Saturday afternoon. However, the fear created by false images conjured up in my head were countered by reality. I knew what I had to do, so now was the time to muster up my courage. This was the right thing for me, even though it was contrary to what I was conditioned to believe. I knew I was surrounded by very competent people in an atmosphere that provided the safe means to do what was necessary for the continuance of my life. I was comforted, knowing this was the correct decision for my best good.

My doctor was not much older than me. Somehow that helped, knowing that he was a contemporary in my age group. He was kind and gentle with an effortless way that put me at ease. He carefully described the procedure and explained exactly what he was going to do in great detail. He assured me that, if I experienced any pain, I could request additional anesthesia.

I put up a tough facade, but underneath I was terrified. For six weeks I had shoved my emotions deep inside so I could proceed with my decision to let go of my baby. Suddenly, here I was at the moment of truth, lying virtually naked in an abortion clinic, about to carry through. In these overwhelming moments, I just wanted to get it over with. I believed, if I could just survive the procedure, my problem would be solved, a hard lesson learned. I had no idea just how close death was lurking. How could I possibly imagine that afterward, instead of relief, those old familiar demons of shame and guilt – now joined by grief and regret - would linger to haunt the darkest corners of my conscience? It would take years for me to come to terms with it all.

The nurse sitting next to me monitored my vital signs while the other nurse assisted the doctor. She placed my feet in stirrups as the doctor adjusted the surgical light at the foot of the table. I was all too familiar with what he was going to do. This procedure was essentially the same as when I had the miscarriage, but this time, instead of the child leaving me, I was the one choosing to remove the baby from my body.

I felt pain almost immediately after the procedure began. I told my doctor this, and he quickly administered more anesthetic. From that point, the abortion went quickly and efficiently. The doctor and his assistants worked as if this were nothing more than a simple tooth extraction. I began to relax, believing I'd soon feel the relief I had so longed for, but the anticipated euphoria ended with shocking suddenness. When the doctor removed the fetus, he casually asked, "Do you want to know the sex?"

What did he say? It was such a simple question. I kept hearing it over and over in my mind, like an old scratched vinyl record with the needle stuck in a groove, repeating the words, "Do you want to know the sex?"

I was stunned. His question was completely unexpected. Did I want to know what sex my child was?

I was barely able to speak, but I uttered the word, "No." I sensed that the baby was a girl, but I thought it might quell the blow if I did not know for certain. Although I could not see her, I imagined the doctor holding my tiny baby in his gloved hand, a human being so developed that he could identify its sex. Suddenly, what had been "a condition" that needed simple surgery to correct became a human being – *my child* whose life I had just destroyed.

Oh my God! This was my baby! What did I just do?

It was done. Over.

Chapter Three

The Next Dimension

A monitor suddenly blared, and I recall the nurse's voice.

"We're losing her!"

I remember the shock in her eyes – the shrill alarm echoing in my consciousness. Then, everything faded. I effortlessly slipped away, the room disappearing into darkness. It was very fluid and easy. I knew what was happening to me. I felt no fear. It all seemed perfectly normal, because, unbelievably, I had been here *before*!

Just a few months earlier, while driving in a summer thunderstorm, my car hydroplaned at 65 mph. The minute I swerved out of control, I knew that was *it*. This had 'fatal accident' written all over it. I said, "Okay God, I'm yours!"

One minute I was "white knuckling" the steering wheel, headed for the median wall, and the next I found myself in a place of complete freedom, a realm of pure harmony devoid of negativity and judgment. It was as if I had been "beamed up" in the nick of time. I encountered entities of color and light, without human form, but with the essence of familiarity, as if we all knew each other. In this realm I felt safe, protected and welcome. Instantly, I knew my life was significant.

Then I heard a voice ask, "Do you want to stay or go back?"

Without hesitation, I chose to return. Why? I wasn't sure, because if this was indeed death, it was beyond any level of perfection I could have ever imagined. But I chose to return, and so, that was that.

Suddenly, I was back on the highway. My car was demolished, but somehow I was still in one piece. The experience left me in awe of how near to death I was. And now, in the abortion clinic a few months later, my body was going into shock and my blood pressure was dropping. Death was calling me again.

I recognized it. It was easy. I had returned to the same ethereal sphere I encountered during my crisis on the highway. It was like coming home to my self again. Welcoming me once more were the spiritual entities of varied shapes and colors, but this time one of them stood out among the others – a particularly loving being. I would not realize its importance until years later. And again, the question was asked. "Do you want to stay or go back?"

Here I was, for the second time, in the midst of the ultimate experience of eternal awareness, something that most of us never experience in a lifetime. Yet, without hesitation I quickly responded, "Yes, I want to go back. I have too much yet to do!"

It was not an audible voice that spoke to me, and my answer was not a verbal response. This was my intuitive guidance and insight that manifested as peaceful understanding, tranquility, and wisdom beyond words or thought, where the question and the answer are one.

In the snap of a finger, I was back. No one in the room knew I had departed. I shifted from infinite awareness, undefined by time and space, to the confinement of the surgical room. The bright, clear colors of the ethereal realm faded to dim shades of gray, as the luminous atmosphere succumbed to the glaring surgical light at the foot of the table.

A wave of panic washed over the room. The nurse quickly put an oxygen mask on my face and gave me an injection. Frantically, the doctor grabbed my legs and lifted them high above my heart. It all happened in a flash. I was between the wonderment of the endless and timeless realm with nothing but good present, and the harsh reality of my medical emergency. And then, just as quickly, the wave receded.

"Her eyes are clearing!"

The nurse's words and the relief on her face made me realize I had returned . . .

What happened to me?

Just an hour ago, I had walked into the clinic with the intention of tying up my problem, neatly packing it up, and hiding it on a shelf where no one would ever find it. Instead, I opened up Pandora's Box.

Something greater within me wanted to return. I didn't have to come back. *I chose to.* I believe I came back to do something that I knew was very important; something that only I could do.

Everything happened so quickly. What I thought was an easy fix to a problem created a more complex journey into the next chapter of my life. It was difficult to comprehend the magnitude of what just took place in the time it took to snap my fingers. But one thing now dominated my conscience. Despite all of the justifiable reasons for my abortion, the price for saving my own life came at the expense of my child's life.

At the same time, my near-death experiences gave me new perspective on what life meant beyond what I knew up to that point. The universe had literally thrown me a lifesaver from the next dimension. But, as is often the case when someone is saved from the brink, they sometimes return to an entirely new and potentially unfamiliar way of life. I didn't realize it just yet, but I had instantly acquired awareness of what it meant to be independent of the world of effects as I once knew it. I felt absolutely free, liberated from anything that confined, defined, and limited me. I had instantly attained what I know as enlightenment, where I was in the full presence of what I call the Divine. The problem was it would take years for me to recognize and understand how to better my life for it.

I just had the most astonishingly meaningful experience I could possibly have imagined, while at the same time the most horrific moment of my life – all in a flash, an instant, a flicker. This was too overwhelming to adequately process on any level. The fear of being "found out" for the pregnancy and abortion trumped what I might have learned from my near-death experience. I tuned out the brilliant golden light of the aware state and instead receded into the darkness that enshrouds abortion. My life had changed overnight.

Shame and guilt were now joined by my newest demon, regret. I quickly fell back on human nature's most formidable defense mechanism: denial. To deal with all that occurred, I tried to forget what I had done. I convinced myself I could go on with my life as it was before the pregnancy, providing I put this behind me. Chalk it up to bad decisions and a lesson learned. Be wiser with my choices, and don't ever let it happen again. Forget it, lock the secret in the vault and move on.

Instead, over time I sank deeper into the abyss, trying to keep my secret from rising to the surface. The harder I tried to force the abortion from my memory, the more it would pop up in ways I never expected. It was like trying to force a beach ball under water. You can't hold it down forever because the inevitable force of nature will wear you down. The ball will eventually overpower you and explode to the surface.

As far as my abortion, I did what I had to do. I had no choice if I wanted to live. But what I tried to force under the surface was the denial of my taking responsibility for ending the life of my baby so I could go on. I knew I made an extremely courageous choice to let her go, but I didn't want to deal with the full ramification of my decision. Additionally, it didn't matter if it was due to unfortunate decisions, by natural circumstances, or at my own hand, the harsh reality was, I was never going to be a parent. How was I going to get around that?

Unfortunately, it didn't take long for the pain and grief to come crashing to the surface. I would burst into tears while watching a movie that included the birth of a baby. I was uncomfortable around young mothers. If I needed something in the grocery aisle that included baby food and diapers, I would put it off until the last of my shopping. I always found an excuse to politely decline invitations to baby showers or a toddler's birthday. Just observing children laughing and playing depressed me. Unbelievably, for years I thought this was a normal existence.

Often, when we fear emotional pain, we don't realize that running from, rather than working through it creates even more misery. An open wound festers and becomes infected if it isn't properly treated and given air to heal. I believed I could steer clear of my grief by denying it. Instead, my resistance perpetuated the very pain I was trying to avoid. Making matters worse, I didn't reach out. I didn't talk about my abortion to anyone, not even Clare, my best friend who was with me that day. I came from a family that didn't talk about personal matters, especially the taboo subjects of sex, pregnancy, and abortion. And so, on I went, struggling to hold that ball of denial under the water and growing more and more weary.

Chapter Four

Grief

Deep emotion experienced in the aftermath of abortion is a form of grieving. Most of us think we grieve only when we acknowledge the death of someone we have known, but whenever we experience any type of loss, we also experience grief. It involves five stages, as first acknowledged by Elisabeth Kubler-Ross[1]. They may not show up in the same order, and some of the stages may repeat themselves as layers of grieving unfold.

Stage one of grief is denial. Stage two is anger. Stage three is bargaining. Stage four is depression, and the final and fifth stage is acceptance. Many of us are unaware that we are in the grieving process. It occurs

[1] Kubler-Ross, Elisabeth. *On Death and Dying*. New York: Macmillan Publishing Company, 1974

whether we are conscious of it or not. If we are not aware, however, we can wallow in one or more of the stages indefinitely.

I can speak for myself when I tried to forget my abortion; I lived in denial for many years. I stuffed the memory so far down that I also did not remember the near-death experience that occurred at the same time. I forgot, until it began to surface in forms that did not appear to be about abortion. I did not acknowledge the grief until the occurrence of several losses over five years. It was as if I had to lose most everything I knew in order to reveal what I had buried.

After the death of four very close family members including my father, the loss of my business and my marriage, putting down five of my six animals due to old age and ill health, and the suicide of one of my closest friends, I finally grieved the loss of my baby. It took the extreme grief of my many losses to bring me to absolute surrender, uncovering the grief of my abortion, which I had buried years before. I was clearly in denial all those years.

Anger, the second stage, showed up in many ways over the years. I stuffed that, as well. It was not until the losses gained momentum, one on top of the next, did I begin to feel the fury. I lost my innocence. My sense of integrity was compromised because I held the deep secret of the abortion for years. I felt I had been living a lie, keeping the nasty secret buried deep within. There was no chance for me to be a mother. My health held me back from that opportunity. I was mostly angry with myself for having ill health – angry with my body.

I was angry with God, whom at the time I thought was punishing me. I felt forsaken and forgotten. My self-hatred stunted my spiritual growth. I had little hope and virtually no faith in the unseen. This hatred diminished my life force, like a disease corroding the good from my being. The anger created the victim attitude of sadness and fury, diminishing me to nothingness. It ate away at my heart and kept me from loving myself or anyone else.

A friend suggested that I take a baseball bat and hit a tree to vent my anger. Being a lover of nature, I couldn't possibly take it out on a tree. So, I bought a toy bat with a spongy covering. I spent many angry moments whacking the bed with my little pink bat, taking out my frustration. No trees were harmed, and no one but me knew of my crazy wrath taken out on my mattress. Oddly enough, it made me feel better and less victim- ized. I released my anger, which I left in the layers of cotton batting, clear down to the box springs. This is what crying does for deep-seeded sadness. It was cathartic and a healthy way to purge the frustration.

The bargaining and anger stages interchanged for years. Sometimes I didn't know the difference. The perpetual rumination, feeling guilt, shame, and regret was a form of bargaining – the third stage. If I could just feel bad enough, I would eventually pay the price. Somehow, I thought, by making myself small enough through my shame, I would finally be exonerated of the offense of aborting my baby. It was self-flagellation; torture that continued to make matters worse until I decided that I would no longer play the role of the martyr. The victimization had to stop. Finally realizing how victimized I was, I resolved to move beyond it. It was time to re-frame my past. Surrendering to my emotions allowed me to feel the full force of what I had been hiding.

This is where I started to take action. I began to talk about the abortion, opening up to my feelings and acknowledging the pain. Atonement is a process in which one removes bargaining from the hypothetical, placing it into action. Rather than leaving my fate in God's hands, I took the responsibility for changing my life.

Stage four – depression - was like a mighty tsunami destroying everything in its path. Alongside the grieving for all my other losses, I tossed my abortion into the mix. It took precedence at times. It seemed like I cried for nearly five years. There was so much to cry about. How to deal with everything I had lost was sometimes beyond my comprehension. Only time and the release of persistent grieving would bring relief.

The anger returned from time to time. So, back to the bedroom with my little pink bat I went. The guilt, shame, and regret subsided as I allowed my grief and depression to rise to the surface and ripple away. I finally climbed out of the deep, dark well, determined to never return again.

At last, acceptance took hold. I began to recognize a way of life that I had only dreamt of in the past - one where I was living in joy, helping others and myself to live wholly. Healing became the path. It was the uncovering of what was once buried now revealed as the foundation upon which I built my life. The establishment of my full self enabled me to live in the moment, grateful for what the abortion experience had taught me. I held my head high, moving forward with purpose and accepting all I had endured, because my demons no longer had power. They instead became my teachers. I learned to live in trust and faith, which was somewhere between "what used to be" and "what was yet to come." It became the promise of intention.

What I thought were problems were only my misperception of the facts, my history, and the story I was telling myself. I now acknowledged whatever feeling arose in the moment. I did this over and over. I transformed the guilt, shame, and regret by embracing the emotions, allowing them to wash over me, then releasing and letting them go.

This is how we transform any energy. It is a form of alchemy, to first become the energy, to experience it fully and truly love what it brings just the way it is, and then let it go. We don't wait for someone or something else to free us of the self-imposed tyranny. We must empower ourselves to do this. Alchemy was once thought of as a way to transform base metals into gold. Now, it is realized as a spiritual transformation. We change our perceptions, and at the same time we attain wisdom and enlightenment through alchemical metamorphosis.

I have developed an amazing guided meditation intended to work through the grief and forgiveness process. I call it "The River."

Sit in a quiet place with no distractions. Close your eyes. Breathe deeply three times, clearing your mind of anything that has your attention. Imagine walking in the woods. You notice a path among the trees. Follow the path as it takes you to a clearing beyond the woods. The path continues downward through a field of flowers and grass. The grass sways in the breeze. The colors of the flowers are more vibrant than anything you have ever seen. The fragrance clears you of anything but the beauty and grace of nature. You hear the soft grass swaying in the gentle wind. You notice magnificent snow-capped mountains around the field, pristine and elegant. Keep following the path as it winds down through the peaceful field until you come to an enormous grove of aspen trees. Their leaves, green on one side and silver on the other, wave back and forth in the breeze like a million silver dollars reflecting golden sunrays.

The aspen grove is on the edge of a peaceful stream, shading a grassy area that invites you to stop and take off your shoes. You step into the clear, cool water on the sandy edge of the riverbank.

You didn't notice until now that you have been wearing a suit of armor. This represents the burdens that you carry. You are accustomed to the weight because you have carried it for so long. But now you want to swim in the cool, clear water. It is inviting you to come deeper into the stream, but the suit of armor is so heavy, it will drag you down. You will not survive.

But there is a way out of this dilemma. If you remove the armor piece by piece, you will eventually be able to go into the water. First take off your leggings. One by one, release them into the flow of the stream. Attach something that you need to release to each piece of the armor. It could be pieces of your wounded heart, regrets, a shameful experience, or something you have denied yourself. It could be that you attach forgiveness of someone, or yourself.

As you take off your armor, place it into the stream and watch it flow all the way down until it disappears beyond the horizon. Continue this until every piece is gone, specifically the breastplate that has shielded your heart all this time. Watch it float down the living waters until it is gone.

Now you are standing free of the armor, the guilt, and all that blocked you from your heart's desires. Feel the water wash over your body as you lay in the stream. Play in the water like a little child. Laugh and rejoice in your freedom. You are released of all burdens that held you down. Liberation is your way of life from this point forward. Stay as long as you want. Specifically, remember how it feels to be free of what weighed so heavily upon you.

When you are ready, leave the stream. Put on your shoes and walk away from the shade of the aspen trees. Return to the path and walk back up through the field of flowers and grass, past the majestic mountains, and into the woods to return to life again, delivered from what once held you down.

You may at any time return to this place where the aspen trees shade the grass by the river. This place is always available to release your burdens, as forgiveness cleanses you of your grief. This type of meditative practice – going deep into consciousness where issues are ingrained – allows us to recognize and resolve problems that have burdened our lives.

Acknowledging grief allows us to face our fear. It allows us to cleanse ourselves of the old demons of the past. We store grief of unresolved circumstances from early childhood. They build upon each other like uneven blocks, and before we know it we have a mishmash of unstable and unresolved hurts and pains. Often, when we feel an emotional charge, it is one of these old blocks rumbling in our mind. Willingness to face grief is the first step of the journey to liberate ourselves from what makes us feel small.

When grief comes up at an inappropriate time, promise yourself that you will take care of it soon. When alone, sit in a quiet peaceful setting where you feel safe to open up to your grief. Allow your feelings to come forward by recalling what brought them up earlier. Permit yourself to truly acknowledge the pain, allowing the tears to flow. Pay attention to where in your body you sense the emotion. Is it in your solar plexus, in your heart, through your shoulders? Just feel it. Wear it. Allow the tears to rise and wash over you. Cry as loud as you want. Feel the grief shaking your shoulders, allowing it to pour out of where you stored the pain and suffering. Give yourself three to five minutes to get it out. Really let it go. Shake it off – literally shake off the grief, then step away and go about your day. This is one of the greatest gifts you can give yourself. When grief arises again, allow it to come to the surface. Let it flow through. Then release it; freeing yourself from what has built up inside. Letting go is one of the most difficult things to do. It takes courage.

Most of us are challenged with attachment. We hang on for dear life, thinking that we are honoring our grief. We think that it is some sort of penance that must be paid. If we don't grieve and suffer enough, we think we are not honoring what we are supposed to remember. But it is not the sorrow that we are to remember. We must acknowledge what we learned from this experience. What did we take from this to enhance our lives? How can we go forward with a greater purpose, utilizing what we have learned from this situation? So, how do we let go and move on?

The word *health* is derived from *wholth*, an Old English word, meaning 'to be whole.' Healing is to transcend suffering. It does not mean that we are pain-free or without scars or challenges. What it does mean is that we rise above the challenge to excel to greater heights from what has gone on before. We take the suffering, move beyond it, and transform it into something better. This way we let go of the lesser to make room for the greater. One way to know if you're healed is by recognizing that you are no longer grieving.

The key to living life well is to know that we are whole, just as we are. All that has happened up to this point has brought us to where we are. There are no mistakes and no coincidences. Whatever we are involved in, whatever conditions we experience, we are within the world that we created for ourselves.

We live in a holographic universe. Out of the choices we make, and from the perceptions we hold, we design the texture and color of life's outcome. What we experience along the way brings us what we need, in this moment, to help rise to our purpose. Our concept of self is what we mirror back, continually manifesting our self-concept.

To transcend suffering is to be content with what is in our existence right now. Suffering is the belief that what we need is different than what we have - accepting the illusion that we are not okay as we are. If we are struggling, it is because we are not in alignment with the laws and principles of life. Once we are in alignment, we are no longer held back. If it is not what we desire, and if our life is challenged, we are at choice to make changes for the better. We surrender what is not working for what is healthier and more whole. This is how we heal.

Sometimes, all it takes is to change our perception, and the holographic universe shows us a different picture. The question to ask is – what is it that I need to know in this moment? What is it that I need to learn? How can I take these circumstances to create something better for my life?

Chapter Five

James

On a recent vacation to the northern shore of Kauai, I was so taken by nature's magnificence. We stayed in a lovely place on the cliffs at Princeville, near the island's stunning Na Pali coastline. When the sun is not impeded by the clouds, the ocean several hundred feet below is bathed in various shades of turquoise, teal, iolite, and indigo. The waves rise and fall, breaking over the ancient lava flow in frothy white foam, and then receding in peaceful tranquility.

Several times each day, fast moving vertical sheets of rain from the northeast interrupt the variant greens of the island and brilliant blues of the ocean. The crisp colors of nature's tropical splendor are filtered by a veil of misty rainfall. What is otherwise apparent in colorful display is rapidly muted in mundane gray. The quick-ening storm's spray also has power over the symphony of ocean waves crashing upon the reef. The sound of the breakers has no recourse but to surrender to the staccato rainfall. Upon the ocean's surface a vivid full rainbow left me feeling like a child viewing nature's awe-inspiring magnitude for the first time.

The whales were returning to the islands after a several months journey from the north. Dozens of dolphins encircled the reef, evenly paced, with an occasional spinner breaking the surface. Life-giving moisture enlivened the red volcanic mountainsides covered with plush emerald green velvet. No matter what the weather, nature's beauty is infinite. At night, the break in the clouds revealed a vast cosmos. Innumerable crystal reflections danced across the infinite dome of deep blue lapis. I surrendered to the darkness in awe and reverence of its obscure mystery.

Nature moves forward on the frothy edge of evolu-tionary advancement, telling its story through repeti-tive fractals of time and space. Our lives are very much in harmony with nature. Human patterns repeat until we decide to make a change. Just as the misty gray of a rainstorm temporarily obscures familiar colors and sounds, we are sometimes so overwhelmed by a problem that we can't see the full spectrum of alternatives or answers. Storms give us a time of waiting; a pause to observe. The suspension of time and space allow us to linger long enough to hear the whisper of wisdom. The answers always lie within the question. The solution is within the problem itself. What lies beyond the veils of gray are the true colors and textures of the full spectrum of life. Even within the darkness of night there are crystals of clarity reflecting light. When we recognize these greater truths, we begin to heal . . .

James and his girlfriend Lori graduated from college in the late 1970s. Lori had just been hired as a schoolteacher, and James went to work as a professional musician in a successful local rock band. They were pursuing their lifelong ambitions, and the world offered all possibilities. And then, Lori became pregnant. Both James and Lori believed that if they had the baby, they must get married, being the children of their parents' generational expectation of moral and ethical behavior. But marriage was not in their plans at the time, nor was parenthood part of the mix.

"We felt like the world suddenly caved in on us," James sadly recalled. "I wanted to be a rock star, not a husband and father. Lori was just starting her teaching career, and she didn't really want to have a child right then. Although we'd been together since high school, we weren't ready for marriage. Lori was very mature, but I was still an adolescent – a wild child playing in a rock 'n roll band. I thought that maybe I would get married someday, way down the road, but I never wanted children."

James and Lori's dilemma was further complicated by self-imposed expectations. "It was 1977, and we were good kids from good upper middle class families. Sure, it was the era of hippies and Free Love, but good little girls and boys just didn't get pregnant. Ridiculous as it sounds now, my first reaction was selfish shame – what will my parents think? What will her parents think? I thought I had them conned into believing I was a level-headed young man, when in fact I was a spinning top in the world of sex, booze and rock-and-roll. Now my girlfriend was pregnant, and I was about to get busted. Pure, white-hot panic. It was all about me. Yes, I was concerned about Lori's welfare, but in reality my biggest concern was, how was this going to affect me?"

Adoption may have been in the back of their minds, but it was not a practical choice. "I don't think we ever discussed adoption," James recalled. "Again, that would mean facing our parents and admitting we weren't perfect; that we, God forbid, had sex without being married. Adoption also meant that Lori would have to give up her new job and go through a pregnancy, only to let go of our baby. For me, I couldn't just run off and join the circus, leaving her single and pregnant. The band was on the road frequently, and I never knew where I was going to be from one week to the next."

Abortion seemed to be the only answer to solve their dilemma.

"I was terrified," James told me. "But at the time, we did what we thought was the right thing."

James said he supported Lori throughout. "I remember the night before we went to the clinic. I don't think I'd slept a wink since we got pregnant, but this night was the worst. I had all these mind-images of back-room abortions, like that Rasta woman in *In the Heat of the Night* who fixed pregnant girls on some dirt floor shanty with roosters and chickens running around. It's crazy, since abortion was already legal then, but I was still terrified that Lori could die. For once, at least, I wasn't just thinking about myself."

James took Lori to the clinic and found an entirely different scenario. "In those days you didn't run into whacko fanatics throwing blood on people outside the clinic. This was no different than walking into any doctor's office. Although I was doubled-up in fear while I waited, the procedure went quickly, without a hitch. I came into the room and sat with Lori while she regained her strength, and then we hopped into the car and went home. Simple, easy, problem solved."

Lori's physical recovery from the abortion went just as smoothly. "I took care of her for several days afterwards," James said. "I was like a mother hen. It was probably the first time in my life that I took responsibility for anything. Man, I thought I was Mother Teresa. But I was clueless. I've looked back on it over the years, and especially now, I can only shake my head. How could I possibly know what Lori was feeling or thinking? After the abortion, I don't think we spoke more than two complete sentences about what happened. I've been told at times in my life that I build emotional walls, and when it came to Lori and our abortion, this one made the Great Wall of China look like a picket fence."

Almost as soon as Lori was well and back on her feet, James said he began to emotionally distance himself. "Somewhere in the back of my mind, I felt like we had done something wrong," he said, "but I didn't want to deal with it. I wanted to forget about it and move on."

Lori went back to work, and James hit the road with his band. But suddenly, within months, he abruptly ended the relationship. "I moved on, alright," he said. "I ran away in full stride – in full denial. I'll never know if our relationship would have lasted, but I put up my wall and never gave it a fair chance, because by staying with Lori I would have to reconcile with something far more serious than our accidental pregnancy. My girlfriend was pregnant with our child. Now, suddenly, she wasn't. I shut down and refused to talk about, or even think about the impact the abortion had on us. Yes, I was physically present for her during the first stage of our crisis, but in the aftermath of grief, when she needed my emotional support, I disappeared."

James put the abortion aside, and life went on. Or so he thought.

He played in the band for four years, but as is often in life, sometimes dreams are trumped by reality. The disco era put many live bands out of work, and James' band went through the typical transient changes endemic to the profession. Eventually, they were replaced by the disc jockey with a disco ball and a collection of vinyl, and it was time for James to once again "move on."

"Suddenly, the work dried up, and most of the guys I played with were getting real jobs," James said. "I had to re-evaluate where I was going. Although I was a pretty good guitar player and singer, I also had a passion for writing. I needed to choose, to commit to working hard and going for the big time in music, or settle down in a more secure world and focus my energy on writing. I guess I was beginning to grow up, because I decided my chance of being a 'star' was a long shot. I was more likely destined to be playing in honky-tonk bars when I was fifty. I was okay with giving up music, but I had to deal with the loss of my childhood dream."

Through James' young life, alcohol was his way to deal. Alcohol helped him cope with shyness, but made him hide from responsibility. It brought out the comedian; the happy-go-lucky guy people loved to laugh with. It dissolved his inhibitions and fueled the dynamic entertainer who delighted audiences. Unfortunately, alcohol also helped him selectively forget certain painful memories. But alcohol did not help him hide from the deepest pain.

"Sure, I was disappointed that I wasn't going to be the next Elvis," James said. "But I got over it. I was doing other things, still a party-hardy boy, and for a time I thought I was doing well. But something was wrong, something more than just the losses and changes that most every young person experiences from time to time. Something was eating at me. Now and then I'd slip into a dim depression, and I didn't know why. I'd heard about older guys hitting midlife crisis at fifty, but I was barely in my thirties. How could I be whining about lost opportunities when I was in my prime?"

A series of recurring dreams persisted. They made no sense to James at the time. Such is the defense mechanism of our memories when ruled by a wounded and unhealed heart. It was not long before the dreams were speaking a loud and clear message of what needed to be healed.

In the dream, Lori was inside a house, sitting in a rocking chair with a baby boy on her lap. James stood outside, peering through a window. No matter how hard he pounded on the window, Lori and the baby did not hear or see him. There was no door for him to open. James would panic, pounding and calling out, but unable to get inside the house. And there the dream would end.

"I'd wake up exhausted and sometimes in utter sadness," James said. "Believe it or not, I didn't get it at first. I was completely bewildered. I had thought about Lori now and again - we stayed in touch over the years – but as ridiculous as it sounds, I couldn't figure out why I was dreaming about her, or who this little baby was, sitting on her lap. I must have had this same dream a dozen times, but the obvious metaphor escaped me. Finally, I guess my mind had enough of my utter denial. The next time I had the usual dream, this one ended with my death – I felt a violent explosion, and I died. When I woke up, it was like somebody hit me with a baseball bat."

He finally understood the dream. He suddenly realized the price he paid for his ambitions was the abortion of his baby. "I'm shut out, looking in and unable to get to Lori and the baby, and then I'm dead. Not only did I realize at that moment that I had abandoned someone I cared for just when she needed me most, I also felt like I sacrificed my child for some crazy pipe dream that never materialized," James said. "The words, 'I killed my baby' ripped through my head. I couldn't have felt any worse if I had gotten the news that someone I loved had just died."

James spent the next three days in isolation. Never before had he experienced such deep depression. For the first time in six years since the abortion, he was grieving. Up to that point, he told no one about the abortion. Not even his closest friends knew. And despite his initial epiphany, it would take a long time before he could speak to anyone about his sorrow and shame.

Change was in the air. James was flying headlong into the heart of the storm. The cold and gray misty veils were just beginning to appear. It was up to him to either work through to the other side, or be consumed in grief, shame, and regret. He began to work through his grief by journaling.

"I had already written a novel a few years earlier," James said, "and I suddenly found myself writing a new story, rather than random journal entries. Before long, this new novel became an obsession."

He spent every spare minute on the book. Among numerous challenges, the novel's main character faces the pain of his participation in an abortion. James spent over a full year writing the book and working through his demons at the same time.

"I believed that completing the novel was the beginning of atonement," he said. "Forgiveness was going to be much harder, but I had to start somewhere." He dedicated the book to Lori.

He sent her a copy of the manuscript, with a letter of apology attached. James and Lori had managed to maintain a distant friendship since the breakup, but they had never discussed the abortion. When she received the letter, she was taken aback, to say the least, but it opened the door to a meaningful dialogue. Through a series of letters, they discussed their loss of innocence and the wounds that had left them both scarred. Lori was able to express to James how she thought that all those years he had been unaffected by the abortion. She now knew differently. Distant wounds were filled with shared sorrow, linking the past pain with a balm of empathy and compassion. All it took was the simple opening of dialogue for the healing to begin.

"It was a double-edged sword," James said. "I felt guilt and shame for breaking off the relationship so soon after the abortion - guilt for rejecting her without an explanation. I could only apologize and beg her forgiveness, but the other edge was forgiving myself for taking my child's life. Lori faced that same challenge. Individually, we were both going to have to deal with that. I can't speak for her, but it's taken me more than thirty years to work through it. I think initially, Lori was more forgiving of me than I was. In fact, after my initial stage of grief, I experienced everything from frustration with myself, to pure self-loathing."

Soon after James faced his demons and began the journey to self-forgiveness, he abandoned the trappings of self-medicating with alcohol. "It's amazing how depression goes away when you stop taking depressants," he laughed. "I discovered I can be confident without crossed eyes."

James has gone on to become an accomplished published author of four novels – one of which is the book he wrote as a catharsis for the guilt of his past. He is now an editor for another aspiring writer, continuing to share his gift of writing through the wisdom developed from facing and moving through his own grief. Additionally, James opened and solicited for donations to a college investment fund to benefit the children of a childhood friend who died at 48. This was another way to give back to the memory of the child he never fathered.

"I was flying blind, but I knew I was heading in the right direction when I first opened up and talked to Lori about the abortion," he said. "I couldn't change the past, but I could affect the future. Finally, at some point recently, I told myself, that's it - I'm paroled. I'm done with the guilt. I forgive me. It's amazing how liberating life can be when you cut yourself some slack for being human."

Lori married the love of her life and became an

"instant mother" to her husband's three children. They have both taught high school for over three decades, Lori dedicating herself to teaching and counseling young adults. Now, over thirty years since the abortion, Lori and James remain dear friends.

Intentionally facing the pain of abortion allowed James to see through the veils of gray that clouded his view for that time in his life. Perhaps James would have become the accomplished man he is today without the experience of the abortion, but it also could be that the gray veil appearing as the storm of abortion caused him to take notice, to observe his life's direction. Once he fulfilled the dream of playing in a band, he chose a different path, one that took him toward a more meaningful way of life.

Now, at this time, looking back on the value of his experience he has learned to recognize the patterns of the storm before they come into view. "We were young, just kids," James says. "It's a bad excuse, but it's the only one I have. I only wish we'd had someone to talk to before we made the decision to have an abortion. We were ashamed and afraid to go to our parents for help. We had three older brothers and a sister between us, yet we didn't even consider reaching out to them for advice. It was that old bugaboo about premarital sex and pregnancy.

"But I often think about thirty-some years of occasional sleepless nights, the nightmares, the tears and pain associated with anything involving children, and the depression at holidays. I don't know if it would have made a difference, but if someone back then told me I would live so long with shame and regret, maybe I might have considered some alternatives to abortion."

James, like many with whom I've spoken, is caught in the middle of the abortion debate. "I don't believe that the feds can deny a woman's right to have an abortion, but I'm not comfortable with the procedure as the end-all to a problem. In many cases, however, I agree that it's a woman's only alternative. Sometimes, even when there are clear and workable alternatives, it may still be the right choice. But I don't deny that Lori and I willfully ended the life of our child, and no amount of debate over when a fetus is 'viable' is going to change that fact. We had an abortion because having a baby wasn't convenient for us at the time. It wasn't right, it wasn't wrong; it was the decision we made, and that's it. We had to live with the choice we made, and deal with the consequences. Other people may not struggle with that, but we did."

The veils of gray, often quite brief, are easy to recognize when we know what to prepare for and how to respond with wisdom. We can wait for them, observe them for what they bring, and let them go, knowing that what lies beyond is life-giving in its varied forms. By acknowledging this, we mindfully traverse the leading edge of our evolutionary becoming. A full view allows the mystery of what the darkness brings, a pinpoint of crystal clarity, and the vivid brilliance of the full spectrum of life.

Chapter Six

Re-membering
Through Forgiveness

Forgiveness is a powerful process in letting go of anger, shame, regret, or any host of past burdens. When we are caught up in our grievances, we can't release our grip on unhealthy, negative emotion. I once heard, "not forgiving someone is like drinking poison and expecting the other person to die." We perpetuate the problem by hanging onto debilitating grief or anger, often to the point of blind obsession.

It reminds me of a time when I was about twelve years old. One of my chores was mowing the grass. We had a lawn mower with an aluminum bottom on the grass catcher. It was an old mower with an exposed spark plug on the top of the motor.

You guessed it.

I took off the catcher while the mower was still running. It was filled with moist grass. The weight was too much, and I touched the metal catcher to the spark plug. It was enough of a shock to make me grip the catcher even more tightly, as if I was frozen to it. I convulsed for quite a while until I finally yanked away and fell back on the grass. The neighbors probably got a big kick out of it.

We tend to grip onto the emotional charge of pain, unable to let go. What we do out of fear is based on our perception of reality. By hanging on, our reality of the past becomes distorted through the veils of time. We hang on, clinging to the pain as if it is a badge of honor.

Remember when you were a child playing the game called "Gossip"? One person would start a sentence, whispering it to another. By the time the last person revealed what she thought she heard, the original sentence had been extremely altered. Everyone laughed at the difference. It is the same with the painful stories we hang on to. Over time we add on, accentuating the offense, until it becomes something entirely different – exaggerated or entirely blown out of proportion. The simple act of forgiveness can release our white-knuckled grip on these illusions, once we finally yield, surrender, and resolve to 'let it go.'

Self-forgiveness, whether we were actually involved in a painful experience, or merely drawn in by our own perception, may be the only process necessary to set a positive path. After all, the offense occurred only from our own perspective. It may not even be perceived as an offense to someone else. Successful forgiveness of the self often exonerates the other party. Compassion for the self transfers to everyone else involved.

It comes down to accountability. I had floundered for several years, blaming people and circumstances for my wrong turns and dead ends. I finally decided that it was time for accountability. No more blaming my parents for what they did or did not do. Pointing my finger at ex-husbands and old boyfriends for my misery only meant that my three other fingers were pointing at little ol' me. It was also time to stop the self-judgment and recrimination. Settling for being just good enough was no longer – good enough.

I decided to go for the best life that I could imagine – to take responsibility for my shortcomings and take credit for my triumphs. As a very intelligent, talented, and good woman, I set the stage for my best life, knowing that I deserved it. I attended numerous classes to seek a breakthrough, to get to the core of my heart. Counseling and reading hundreds of books helped me overcome my barriers.

I learned that facts are only evidence of what occurred in the past, being the effect of previous causes, but they are not necessarily the inevitable portent of things to come. I had to clarify the difference between the facts of my past and the truth of who I am. I began to understand that placing my attention upon my truth shifted the process by which the universe responded to my life. A higher order began to take hold. I learned to shift my attention from my outward perspective of being a victim, to within, where my place of power resides. This created a place of harmony and self-confidence. The ancient Greeks believed to be beautiful was to be in harmony with the universe, and to do that, we must first be in harmony with nature.

As a child, I was taught to do the right thing. I learned to make moral decisions. Being human is about choice. We cannot take conscious, educated choice out of the equation. This is what separates us from animals that operate by instinct alone. As humans we discern, judge, and decide through conscious choice, and thus we are responsible for the outcome of our lives. Thoughts become responses and reactions, resulting in choices – or decisions based on choice. If you desire different results, you must first change the cause – the thought. If you change the way you choose to think, the results respond in a different way, dependent upon the choices made. Our results come from our thoughts.

What I have learned over the years is that what is right for me, as I choose for my life's path based upon the facts of the present and past events, is not necessarily the right choice for someone else. Their circumstances are different than mine. The choices we make are based upon the context of our own circumstances. There is very little that occurs in our lives that we cannot control; how we respond determines outcome. We live by the law of cause and effect. For me, the simple fact was, the choices I made, and my responses to them, affected the outcome of my life. My life began to turn around once I rejected the old, and generated new and more positive thoughts and self-perceptions. Bad choices equal bad outcome. Good choices equal good outcome. It might sound rudimentary and simplistic, but it often takes many of us the better part of a lifetime to get it.

The Universe is always conspiring for our good. When I finally understood what that meant, I began to go with the flow instead of pushing back the waves with a broom. We often learn our greatest lessons while navigating through our most difficult challenges. If we work through it effectively, we will not have that particular type of challenge again. We then move forward in the direction of our dreams with a more graceful and an easier way of being.

I made the decision to have an abortion for my best good. I chose circumstances that gave me back my life. I made the best choice that I could, under the circumstances at the time, so I could move forward with the highest intention for living fully. Accountability arises out of courageous choice, creating a way of life that allows us to follow our truth.

Baggage is a common term for the nagging aspects of our past that we carry. If that baggage were a literal object, it would grow heavier as we weaken under the weight. Over time we force ourselves to carry more bags to bring all our compiled "stuff" along. Holding a bag for twenty minutes is not such a burden, but consider what it would be like to hold on to it for weeks, or even years. Several bags full of old gripes and complaints become an enormous encumbrance upon our psyche and our heart. There is no room for much else. Forgiveness and accountability gets rid of the baggage.

James achieved self-forgiveness when he finally realized, "If someone else talked to me the way I talked to myself, I would have punched him in the nose. I said, 'I'm a good person, so why am I beating myself up?' It was finally time for me to give myself a break." He began to assess the way he thought and spoke about himself and changed it to self-respect. He realized that he and Lori made the decision to have an abortion in full conscience, and with best intention. He could wallow in regret for the past, or move forward and grow from the experience. He later concluded his actions at the time were wrong, but he made amends and achieved atonement. James is a man of high self-esteem. He now makes choices and decisions with great purpose, intelligence, balance, and tenacity. These are just some of the attributes that he developed as a result of his experience with abortion.

The biblical definition of atonement means to make amends, reconcile, or to be 'at one' with God. We may also atone for what we have done that is incompatible or in disharmony with someone, some principle, or ourselves. I believe this is what our earthly journey is about. We tend to live in separation from God, or our higher self. Eventually, we seek to ultimately rejoin our higher nature. James found his way by courageously facing his demons and letting them go. He became 'at one' with himself.

By releasing our hold on the regret, guilt, and shame of abortion, while transforming it into acceptance and peace, we change ourselves from a victim mentality to one of courage. When we utilize the power of forgiveness, we use our discerning nature that stems from the willingness to seek healing. Healing removes the emotional charge around the pain we once knew. Forgiveness liberates us from the self-imposed shackles of fear, guilt, shame, regret, and grief.

There are many books, classes, and processes available that are dedicated to the subject of forgiveness. I am not going to illustrate a series of exercises to follow, but I will suggest a simple way of forgiveness that works for me. I repeat a mantra, while keeping in mind who or what I am forgiving. I simply say, "I forgive, I forgive, I forgive…" many times over. I use prayer beads, speaking the mantra with each bead, to keep me mindful and in sync. It is simple and effective. When I feel lighter, as if a weight has been lifted, I am done for the time being.

Forgiveness, as we are taught, is the continual process of peeling away layers of the onion. It is written that Jesus taught his apostles to forgive seventy times seven. Literally, this is 490 times. Imagine if we were to forgive ourselves and others that often. All would be cleared of the offense, and there would be nothing left to forgive. His teaching conveyed that forgiveness is continual. It is a form of letting go and an avenue to humility, which clears the heart and mind. It frees us up to feel gratitude for the experience, and to recognize its gifts.

When I began to practice forgiveness for *every* circumstance in which I felt I had been hurt, violated, or abused, my life started to shift. I listed every griev-ance from the time I could remember. It was an enormous list! Had I been able to slice it in half, it would have looked like the Grand Canyon with layer after layer of the varied textures and colors of pain and anguish. It was deep. I had a lot of work to do.

I forgave every big and little incident that caused a story to play over and over in my mind. Attached to those stories were years of beating myself up for my complicity. I might as well have been wearing a neon sign on my forehead, reading, "VICTIM HERE."

The many layers of guilt, shame, and victimization fell away as I began the process to release the pain. I finally took responsibility for how I felt during all those years of carrying around the victim's baggage. No one else but me was to blame, because I chose to hang on to the stories. By taking responsibility for the direction of my life, my consciousness began to shift. I was taking charge in a different way - a means of personal empowerment. I set boundaries that enabled me to speak my truth with self-respect. I learned the word "No." Then I released my attachment to all the pain that had occurred. I forgave myself. I was liberated.

I *re-membered*, piece by piece, assembling myself back into the order of my truth. I discovered that I was blocking not only my fears, but my good memories, as well. As I unpacked and sorted through my emotional baggage, I was able to discard that which no longer served me. My joy returned as I regained faith in myself. I became a woman of courage, living authentically through loving intention and purposeful direction.

For me, one form of spiritual deepening is through the Lakota Inipi Ceremony, or sweat lodge. "Inipi," in Lakota means re-birth. It is a purification or coming into newness as I crawl into the dark dome. It feels like moving into the womb of Grandmother Earth. A few years ago I was invited to a special Inipi Ceremony presided over by Chief Homer White Lance, of the Rosebud Reservation. Struggling with claustrophobia, I sat by the door of the small lodge in case I needed to leave quickly. Through the Chief's guidance, the majority of the ceremony was centered on clearing me of the fear. When I thanked him following the ceremony, he asked, "Are you the woman who was sitting behind me?" I told him I was, and he then said, "Your demons are your problem. You are to look at them, move through them, and let them go." If we move through our fear with forgiveness and gratitude, we surrender to something greater, causing us to release it and let it go.

Today, I no longer have claustrophobia. This advice has become a mantra for me. Whenever I feel fear creating a wedge between my desires and my intended direction, it is an invitation to follow these simple, wise steps.

Our demons are what some people consider being "possessed." They seem to control our lives through the consistent negativity of which we refuse to release. Built up from our fears, from which we run, hide, or attempt to cover, our demons turn into unconscious thoughts and actions, sometimes developing into sublimation and addiction. We think we have solved the problem by blocking or running away. Instead, the problem follows us in a variety of forms. Resistance fuels the fire that won't die until we refuse to feed it. Resistance shows up in our dreams. Our relationships exhibit unhealthy patterns. Bad habits and addictions develop out of the inability to face our demons. Resistance is the invisible painful memory that appears on a movie screen, or sings to us in a popular song, or stalks us in the aisle at the grocery store. Wherever we are, it follows. It is our shadow.

If we turn around and face the shadow, it automatically disappears. When we muster up the courage to face our fears, the illusory boogey man goes away. We no longer have to fight what lurks in the darkness. Mercy and compassion begin to grow when grace replaces the demons of fear. What once possessed us no longer has any power. We let it go – releasing it into greater possibilities. In turn, we are liberated from the burden we have carried. We are free.

Chapter Seven

Rose

Rose grew up in a traditional upper middle class New England family. Her father ruled the household with an iron fist. He was the dominant force of the family. Possessing the wisdom and intelligence of an old soul, Rose grew up the middle child with three sisters and a brother. She had a strong work ethic and high integrity.

During her young adult years, she fell in love with a guy who at first seemed to be a good young man, but after a time, a pattern of emotional abuse emerged. Rose had a tender heart. She was a peace-maker, gentle in nature. In order to deal with the overpowering energy of her boyfriend, she felt it was best to back down and stay as invisible as possible. What most of us don't realize is that 'doormat energy' is the flip side of the bully. It took two very hard lessons for Rose to resolve that she would no longer allow any man to wipe his feet upon her.

Rose got pregnant after dating her boyfriend for one year. They decided the best way to handle the situation was to have an abortion. Afterwards, just when she was healing and trying to cope, she became pregnant again. Mortified, Rose faced another horrible decision. The last thing she wanted was to have a child who would bind her to this abusive young man.

Unfortunately, we sometimes have to undergo extreme circumstances to recognize the challenges of what we no longer want in our lives. It is one of the unfortunate symptoms of abusive relationships. Victims often don't recognize that they are in a pattern of abuse until it becomes extreme. Tolerance is a way of life. Kindness of others is always suspect. The timid child becomes the wary adult who waits for the bully to show up around every corner. Trust is not a common attribute of abuse survivors. Rose wore the shield of one who has experienced such cruelty, keeping others at arm's length to protect herself from further mistreatment.

Back then, when making some of the most extremely difficult decisions of her lifetime, Rose had no one to turn to. Her family was not equipped to give her advice. "I was raised in an atmosphere of, 'don't let the neighbors know,'" Rose said. Her mother never taught her the facts of life. There were no social organizations or family planning clinics that offered information or help in considering her options. Making the best decision that she could at the time, with what little information she had gathered on her own, Rose chose abortion again.

Prior to the procedure, a counselor at the clinic spoke with Rose to make sure she was prepared to follow through. Very little counseling was offered, however. The 'counselor' simply provided a small checklist of questions for Rose to answer. Rose said the entire process felt very mechanical to her – that it seemed like the counselor was doing nothing more than covering all the legal bases before Rose went through with the abortion.

Not long afterwards, Rose severed the relationship with her boyfriend and tried to move on with her life. "I felt very strong about my decision to have the abortion for many years," Rose said. She believed she had made the right choice. But the pain of both abortions hit home years later when she experienced a miscarriage during her marriage to another man. The remorse and regret of her loss became almost too much to bear. At the time, she wanted to be married and have children.

"At forty, following the miscarriage, I left my husband," Rose said. "I made a conscious choice to leave my marriage and not be a mother." Shortly after the divorce, she moved to another state to create a new atmosphere for growth and change. "Being from a traditional family background, it seemed to be expected of me to be a wife and mother, and to have the proverbial house. After many years I reconciled that I was not to be a mother, and I am now fine with that."

She later joined a spiritual community that supported her need for healing. She participated in a number of grief and loss workshops that helped her acknowledge the pain of her losses.

Several years ago, Rose and her sister, who also had an abortion, created a ritual for the children that they released. "We went into our own corners and wrote letters to our children," Rose said. "Then, we made a fire in the wood stove and lit a candle for each child that we lost. We each read our letter out loud, also reading a poem and playing a piece of music. Then we each burned our letter, stating our intentions of letting go." They followed the ritual by sharing some wine.

The performance of ritual generates great spiritual power. Rose and her sister's ritual sealed their losses with a blessing. Burning the letters signified a form of energy transformation, representing purification, cleansing, and the permanence of letting go. It further represented the release of what once was, transforming it into new energy for creation.

At a later time in her life, Rose found herself in the thick of grief that arose from somewhere deep within. Her body had reached perimenopause, a time in a woman's life when emotions run high and it seems everything that needs to be healed comes to the surface. Repressed grief often surfaces when triggered by seemingly innocent comments or events. Rose's "button" was pushed when she heard several women talking about their children.

"It seemed that every time I turned around I heard

women tell stories of their 'miracle baby,'" Rose said. "There was some deep anger there. It was in my face, demanding to be healed. I knew that anger was a healthy stage of grieving. It shows movement through the grief when you say 'Yes!' to the catharsis of letting go."

The loss of her two abortions and miscarriage were clearly still in the process of healing. Sometimes, just when you think you cannot take any more sorrow, healing unfolds. This is the grief process. We face the dark night of the soul in the deepest shadows, revealing our true nature. Only by going through the pain can we heal.

Rose was feeling the ill effects of achiness in her joints, specifically extreme pain in her shoulders. Sometimes strain in the neck and shoulders is an indication of regret and sorrow; the heaviness of grief's weight upon our soul. Rose worked through her grief by allowing it to rise to the surface. She did a lot of clearing work to focus her mind. For Rose, running is a clearing process, as each step symbolically and spiritually moves her farther from her pain. Getting out into nature is an important aspect of healing work. Physical exercise and spiritual practice support our innate sense of self. Rose also practices Yoga.

She says, "It's grounding. It fills me with the power of the earth which gives me strength."

An hour each morning, she meditates and spends time in prayer and study. She uses the shower to allow the water to wash over her, clearing her mind and body of anything holding her back. "The lesson of spiritual practice is not about gaining knowledge," Rose says, "but about how we love – the compassion for self and others."

Rose believes that her grief is now complete. If any triggers arise, her belief system and daily practices continue to bring healing. Rose says, "Spiritual practice is building resiliency, so when you get hit with the unexpected, you've got some sense of self supported by what you deeply believe."

We never lose the innate goodness of our nature. It is a part of the blueprint of life, but regret can overshadow the memory of that goodness. Whatever we experience in our conscious life is our own truth. When Rose first began working with the youth in her church, she felt unworthy, but she worked through the inner demons of this challenge.

"I chose to change the course of my life," she said. "I had to stand up for myself, because I had to make these hard decisions. I had many lessons around loss, and they have made me strong. One of the greatest things I have learned is that 'No!' is a complete sentence."

Based on her resolve, Rose has become a cheerleader for the youth in her church, validating them by helping them build foundations for intelligent and conscious decision-making. Rose shares with each young person, "You are who the world has been waiting for. Your individual gift to the world is waiting to be expressed!" Her loving and tender way wraps itself around each young person she counsels, giving them what she needed when she was growing up – an adult they can trust, one who will listen and not judge.

Rose is involved in a 24-hour retreat for girls. They commune together, creating a safe space, allowing the healing process to unfold and develop. Anchored in safety, trust is established among the girls and young women, furthering an atmosphere of a loving community. Rituals and spiritual practices are part of the experience. The girls are able to openly discuss concerns of the heart from the trust that is established.

Ongoing relationships develop, creating a loving atmosphere that continues over time.

Rose feels her experiences have given her an inner wisdom that enables her to identify with the challenges that young women face. "When I had these big decisions to make, I had no one to talk to," Rose said. "I wish I had more education about contraceptives and alternatives to abortion."

Rose wants to bridge that gap for young people. She has become the adult that she, herself, needed over thirty years ago - a strong yet gentle mentor who speaks frankly, listens intently, and loves unconditionally. Rose has transformed regret and sorrow to love and support, which young people will remember for years to come.

Chapter Eight

Gratitude

Gratitude appreciates. It increases as it takes on its own momentum, for anything of a positive nature generates its own expansion. There is no greater shift in consciousness than being thankful or living in praise. It generates momentum for greater things to come.

When we are appreciative, we are thankful for what is, as a result of what was. Being grateful for all that has gone on in the past enables us to be aware of who we are today. This includes gratitude for what abortion has taught us. We take what was tragic and painful, and honor the lessons we have learned. Gratitude allows us to transform the negative energy of the past to a more optimistic outlook for the future. Instead of saying,

"I'm ashamed of what I did," you can serve yourself better by saying, "I'm grateful for what I have learned, and I am making better choices as I move forward."

Being grateful releases our attachment to fear. Fear cannot expand in the presence of gratitude, for gratitude outweighs negativity. Being appreciative also helps in the forgiveness process, allowing us to recognize the many gifts in our circumstances. Gratitude helps us shift our awareness from what we don't want, to what we have that is good. It develops exponentially as we affirm our appreciation for life. The combination of forgiveness and gratitude is a guaranteed recipe for success when we decide to take life by the hand and move forward.

Keeping a gratitude journal is a good tool for keeping track of what we are grateful for. Before going to sleep, journaling about the day's blessings ends the day on a positive note. It creates a higher consciousness and results in positive dreams. When you wake in the morning, before getting out of bed, consciously be grateful for what the day will bring. Ask, "What is it I am grateful for today?" Remember throughout the day what came to mind. It will set a positive tone as the day progresses.

Gratitude naturally cleanses what is unpleasant from our memory. It is like a murky glass of water. When clean drops of water are consistently dripped into the glass, over time they eventually displace the murkiness with clean, clear water. Gratitude for what you have attracts more of the same. A good way I have found to generate anything I desire is to be grateful for what I already have. I generated my amazing relationship by doing this. I made a list of all the things for which I was grateful. I then listed everything I wanted and expected in a relationship. At the end of the list I added, "This, or what is for my greater good," leaving me open to what was best, without limitations. I read the list every day, sometimes more than once. It was a reminder of what I desired. It cleared murkiness from my mind and opened my heart for the man of my dreams to come into my life.

I did not list what I didn't want, because the universe supplies us with what we focus our thoughts and emotions upon. Our deepest emotions generate more of the same. If we are having a bad day, it seems like everyone else is having one too. But if we shift to a positive frame of mind, it's amazing how it seems that everyone around us changes for the better. Life is a mirror. What we put out, we get back.

Incidentally, I got the great guy, the perfect relationship, and I have never been happier!

Imagine being grateful for what was learned from our experience with abortion. What did it teach me? What has occurred in my life because of that experience? How have I become a better person because of my abortion? What changes did I make because of my experience, and how has that affected others in a positive way? By shifting our perspective, we recognize the continuum from where we have come, to where we are now. We view the journey as our teacher, knowing that we move on to greater things *because* of the experience, not in spite of it.

I now know that I create my life each and every day simply by choosing how I respond to what happens. If I waste my day away with negativity, I might break things, lose my temper, and say something that I typically would not say. My day ends up being one challenge piled upon another. When I set a positive tone by looking at the events of my day as a blessing, my day almost invariably goes well. Of course, life isn't perfect. Things happen. But if you expect positive results, you set every day on a positive track and react well to the unexpected curves life sometimes throws.

These choices are up to us. Ask yourself, who do you choose to spend time with? How do you choose to worship, work, and play? Do your choices serve you, or are you spinning your wheels participating in activities that do not bring you joy and leave you feeling unfulfilled? Choosing mindful living with conscious gratitude fills life with what is expansive, life-giving, and joyful. Tell yourself, "I simply need to change my direction gradually, in small ways, so that my sail is filled by the wind pushing me forward." In a week, a month, and a year, what a difference it will make.

Appreciating the adventure in each day is a form of gratitude. We live in an atmosphere that seeks itself, just as water seeks its own level. This is a principle of physics. What we seek is seeking us. By letting go, we are no longer stuck in the past. The demons have no power. When we face them, our perspective changes from fear to understanding. What we feared becomes strength, built with the courage to move forward. All we have to do is look at the demons, move through them, and let them go. We free ourselves of what has held us back. As we live in appreciation for what we have learned, giving back to others from that experience, we generate a purposeful existence. We no longer think of ourselves as the victim of circumstance. The circumstance is now healed, becoming an enhancement to our life's journey. As we develop through conscious intention, we expand upon the infinite spiral of growth and change.

Through surrender, the letting go of the lesser and opening up to a greater way of being, we become transcendent. But we must first be willing to let go. This is an act of faith. We must be courageous enough to release our hold of what is not in our interest, and trust in the infinite field of possibilities. We do this by living in gratitude for what we have, and trust in our intuition.

Chapter Nine

Fourteen

M y good friend Stephen is a high school counselor. We recently discussed the alarming number of high school students who are faced with the challenge of pregnancy and abortion. He pointed out that, in his experience, young teens and young adults simply lack the maturity to evaluate and understand consequences. He said that the frontal cortex of the human brain does not reach full maturity until around the age of twenty-five. This critical region of the brain, among other things, controls our ability to discern between healthy and dangerous actions, recognize future consequences, and behave responsibly within society.

Stephen explained that this is why many young

people do not seem to have any sense of mortality – why many behave impulsively and often with reckless abandon. Their ability to make critical, sometimes life-altering choices often hinges on their limited ability to decipher and understand consequences. They drive faster, party harder, take enormous risks – they know no boundaries. Younger people, especially teenagers, simply cannot make discerning choices necessary for living life more effectively until they are more mature. A quick look at auto insurance premiums for drivers under age twenty-five bears this out. The accident rate is dramatically higher for this group.

Teenagers and young adults are tremendously challenged with not only scholastic achievement, but familial expectations, financial concerns, and most of all social relationships. Transitioning from childhood to adulthood and all its alchemical processes places high expectations upon youth. Dealing with unwanted pregnancy places a high, if not incomprehensible demand on a teenager's ability to accept responsibility and decipher consequences.

According to Stephen, for most teen pregnancies that he sees, the parents make the decision to terminate. The pressures are so demanding that the decision for abortion must fall upon a responsible adult. Unconditional and non-judgmental support from parents is therefore critical to the child's emotional foundation. As young people, we have all done things that we regret later in life. Some are situations that we laugh off in embarrassment, but more serious things like pregnancy and abortion can send a young girl's self image spiraling into a dark abyss of shame and regret. It is important for parents to establish boundaries for their children, but it's equally essential to create an atmosphere of trust within those boundaries. It is far better to teach a child about consequences with empathy, than to condemn her for them. Passing judgment for an action that a child is intellectually incapable of comprehending creates guilt, shame, regret, and self-judgment that can adversely affect her adult life.

I recently had the opportunity to chat about my book with a gentleman who was speaking at a motivational conference I was attending. When I told him the book was about healing the emotional scars of abortion, his demeanor instantly changed from a polished businessman to someone deeply affected by his own experience. Suddenly, he began to pour his heart out as if we were old friends. I was touched by his immediate emotional vulnerability. He opened up about his wife who, at the age of fourteen, was forced to have an abortion. If I had to guess, I imagine this probably happened sometime in the 1950s.

This poor little girl was virtually branded a modern-day Hester, labeled as a "sinner." She was blamed not only for her pregnancy out of wedlock, but for the abortion that her parents forced on her. She violated the standards, in their eyes, of the age-old limiting belief systems of an extremely conservative and small religious community.

Had she kept the child, she would most likely have been forced to marry the teenaged boy who fathered the baby. What kind of parents would they have been at such a young age? They could have given the child up for adoption, but her family would still bear the shame of their daughter having a child outside of marriage. Instead, to save face, her parents made the decision for her. They chose abortion. Sadly this young girl was made the scapegoat for the shame her parents felt. Instead of supporting her with love and compassion, her parents projected guilt and shame on her, which she carried into her adult life. This man whom she later married told me that she lives with guilt to this day, branded with the proverbial Scarlet Letter. In this case the "A" stands for abortion.

As I learned from my counselor friend, this unfortunate teenager lacked the emotional maturity to discern consequences, so she simply accepted the censure of her family and community. Without loving support, her husband told me, she grew up "emotionally detached, unable to embrace and fully love our own children." Her husband and children have consequently suffered her inability to overcome the guilt and shame that was so unfairly heaped upon her.

"Shame on you!" Do you remember being scolded by an adult shaking his finger in your face? The feelings of degradation and regret can forever sting from the memory of such harsh judgment. What was it that was considered to be so shameful - of dishonor, disgrace, embarrassment, and humiliation? How was it considered to be immoral, which is one of the strongest words defining shame? Immorality is considered to be knowledge within oneself that is contrary to conscience. It is also contrary to divine law, which in the opinion of believers is a rule which comes directly from the will of God.

In the case of the pregnant fourteen-year-old, who was in shame – not honoring divine law? Whose conscience was in question? An innocent girl, who had yet to develop the ability to decipher consequences of her actions? Responsibility was placed upon the girl, but in honest evaluation it was derived from the family and community, as products of their environment, that condemned her. How differently her life might have turned out if she had been treated with compassion instead of judgment.

So how do we grow beyond these judgments? We can choose to take the hand that is dealt us, or we can trade those cards for others that better suit us. We are also at choice to walk away from the game while choosing a different perspective on how to deal with our past. Life offers a multitude of opportunities to reclaim our true nature that are never based in guilt or shame. We do not have to live with the burdens that keep us small.

We stay small when we do not face our inner demons of fear. In the case of this young girl, the voices of the past continue to play in her memory like a broken record. Her fears prevent her from advancing to her greater self. The demons of guilt and shame perpetuate greater challenges. They can have a crippling effect that show up as wounds not yet healed.

When we live in the darkness of fear, where guilt and shame dwell, the stories we build become distorted illusions. Collective belief systems we subconsciously adopt accrue from our limitations. Until we rise above this dwelling place, we cannot move forward. Through thoughtful discernment, we can sift through the falsehoods we are conditioned to believe and shun that which no longer serves us. We then arrive at a place within, where we can expand our conscious awareness.

I'm reminded of the story of the young farmer who bought a new donkey. His old donkey was no longer needed, but the farmer couldn't afford to feed and care for both animals. Instead of selling or giving away the old donkey, the farmer thought he would solve his problem by digging a pit and burying it alive. The donkey would die, and no one would know.

When the farmer shoved the donkey into the pit, it landed on its feet, bewildered and confused. The farmer began to shovel the dirt on the back of the donkey, but the donkey just shook and then stepped up on the dirt. As each shovel of dirt was heaped on the back of the old donkey, he continued shaking it off and stepping up. Higher and higher the donkey rose until it eventually arrived at the top of the pit and walked away.

The moral of the story could be a couple of things: if you attempt to bury your problems they will eventually rise up to meet you. Or, better yet, you can shake off your challenges, creating opportunities to build you up from where you stand. Shake it off and rise above! Perhaps the best lesson – don't ever be the donkey!

If we courageously face our demons, we can rise above what once nearly buried us in darkness. We face the fear and move directly through the illusion of pain. Fear has no power when we confront it. Instead, we arrive at a place where we honor ourselves and create peace within. If we look at the past from a different perspective, we now see it as the foundation built to support our greatness.

Chapter Ten

Riding the Wave

S itting on the beach is one of life's greatest pleasures for me, but my surfing skills leave much to be desired! Once, when I was nineteen, I was washed out with the surf on a rented surfboard. The shore seemed to be an enormous distance away. The tallest buildings on Waikiki Beach looked to be a half-inch high. Having recently watched *Jaws*, I could hear in my mind the orchestra of stringed instruments playing duhm, duhm, duhm, duhm, while I searched for sharks. I was out on the ocean for at least two hours, holding onto the dim hope that the tide would take me back to shore. My white skin was now bright pink, and I was beginning to picture myself instead washing up dead on some distant shoreline.

I finally decided that, if I was going to survive, I had to overcome my fear of the unseen danger below the surface and slip from the safety of my surfboard into the water. So, in I went. I held the board with one arm and began to paddle back to shore. Once I created momentum and began helping myself, the ocean waves pushed me the rest of the way. Talk about a metaphor for life! It reminds me of the advice I received from my Lakota friend – "you must face your demons, move through them, and let them go."

Now I just sit, watching the surfers from the safety of the beach. The surfer paddles directly toward a swell until it breaks. Ducking his head and literally diving through the wave, he swims underneath and through it, eventually rising to the top and paddling on to challenge the next wave. When he paddles far enough, he turns his board around and waits for the big wave. When it comes, he paddles to gain momentum, rises to his feet, and rides the wave back to shore.

To master the waves takes great strength, fortitude, persistence, balance, and a little bit of insanity. It is the insanity that gives the surfer courage to face the wave head on. He moves through his challenge, eventually rising to the top by using the water's power to ride with dominion. This is the turning point of facing our demons; being just insane enough to stop running from the fear, we turn and dive straight in. Fear is the neighborhood bully; he feeds on your reluctance. If you're not afraid to face him, he has no power over you.

When we honor our shadow self - our demons - we rise to the surface with greater wholeness, allowing us to rise above and take charge of our life. We find that the demons are not what we thought they were. They can, in fact, empower us if we learn how to change them from what we fear, to what gives us strength to ride the wave.

Scientists and spiritual leaders alike teach us to shift our thinking into new awareness so that simply by changing our thoughts, we change our life. By letting go of what no longer works, words and actions take on new form, creating a new way of living. Consciously choosing to make changes, and employing positive emotion and enthusiasm with those thoughts, we redirect the brain's ability to rewire. We alter the neural net - the wiring of the brain - activating a new way of thinking and altering our body's responses.

Some say that we can just look at life differently and it will change. It does. It is that simple. Let us not only do that, but let us look at past experiences that brought us pain and re-frame them into a new definition. We then free ourselves of the self-sabotage of past events. The quantum field allows us to make choices from infinite possibilities through our way of thinking and our perspective. We then literally live in transparency, free of past encumbrances. As we let go, we liberate ourselves into a greater sense of our whole being where nothing is shameful. Let us redefine our lives so we can live fully.

My relationships with those whom I love do not end when they die. I just no longer experience what I knew with them in the physical world. When we accept that our lives are not restricted to the simple physical realm, we open up multi-dimensional levels of possibility. In some cases my relationships deepened, and in the case of my baby, our relationship had just begun. I began to ask what this meant for me. I truly had to look into the deep grieving that I continued to feel. My intangible relationship with her taught me a new form of living beyond what the physical world offered.

I was raised in the Christian based belief of

everlasting life. So, if this were the case, I could not destroy my baby's life because she lives in eternality beyond this earthly world. I had personally experienced that very phenomenon twice in my near-death experiences, so why would this not be true for her?

Purposely, I have studied many forms of religion and spirituality to come to a deeper understanding of life and death. Every religion provides varied cultural interpretations of spirituality, but at the heart they are one and the same. There are many paths to God. Our spiral journey up the mountain crosses the paths of many others, ultimately becoming one path to the top. As we live our lives more meaningfully and consciously, we move into a greater understanding that each and every day is about dying to the old self and being reborn into a new realm of what life has to offer. We die each day when we go to sleep. Awakening in the morning is to be renewed for what the new day brings. We must let go of what no longer serves us in order to embrace a fresh existence that broadens our vantage point in the journey to self-fulfillment.

Life is not about acquisition, but about releasing what holds us back from our forward growth and expansion. Life is truly about letting go.

Chapter Eleven

Daniel

We think of abortion mostly in terms of how it affects women. But there are many men who struggle with their complicity, especially after many years have passed.

Now in his early fifties, Daniel tells of when he was twenty years old, working as a carpenter. He had a couple of years yet to finish college before he graduated with his bachelor's degree. He planned to go on to graduate school. He and Lydia had been dating for two years when they found out that she was pregnant.

Lydia was the eldest of five children, raised in the Catholic tradition. Daniel was the eldest of three, with no formal religious background. He says he had no religious baggage, per se, around the subject of abortion. Yet, he said, "We were both immature, without the tools to talk with contemporaries. We were so ignorant. We thought we knew it all and could do it on our own."

He talked about the day of the abortion. With great emotion, Daniel said, "I remember coming home and drawing a bath for her. She just sat in the bathtub and cried." Daniel regretfully said, "To this day, what tears me up about that moment was not having the maturity to hold her in that sacred place. I should have been at her beck and call, in every way, emotionally and spiritually – to really be in the moment for her, and with her, but I wasn't.

"Over the years, Lydia was so burdened by what she held as the guilt brought on by her religious beliefs," Daniel said. "I didn't have that guilt, either as a man or as an individual limited by that religious paradigm. I had no religious tethers tying me to a belief system that force-fed me the guilt so abundant in the Catholic tradition. In this case, I felt strong where she felt vulnerable as a result of her carrying this shame."

They managed to stay together for another year.

"I'm certain that at a subconscious level, she associated me with the abortion," Daniel said. "This is the dynamic of stupidity, when we felt immortal on one hand, and on the other hand there were the pressures of what you are going to be the rest of your life. You make choices out of that dynamic. We eventually broke up."

We all take with us aspects of growth, whether we intend it or not. We grow from making conscious and unconscious choices. But mostly, out of the pain of grief and sorrow, we are unaware that we are pushed into an expansive realm that stretches us beyond our previous understanding until we look back on what caused the pain.

"One thing I learned from this experience was to have greater compassion for others," Daniel said. "I see another suffering, and my heart feels the pain. Out of this experience, in some ways I have limited my own growth, and in others I have grown exponentially. On one end, I think about how I am the end of my family line. That is simply my ego talking. I will not have children carrying on the family name. Yet, I've been able to use my gifts to serve others through my career path. I have used my gifts and strengths to be in service to others, without apology, without regret, and without looking over my shoulder. I have given back to the world in my own way, to my capacity."

Daniel was not affected by guilt or shame as greatly as Lydia. What he did suffer was his not knowing how Lydia fared over the years. "My biggest ongoing thought surrounding the abortion is how she is doing. Because of the way she was raised, she experienced the pain through her guilt and shame that had been heaped upon her by her religious and family background," Daniel said.

He spoke of his eventual reflection upon what took place, because of how we live in regret. His philosophical viewpoint, well stated was, "All that time we spend trying to bury it and were subsequently not living in the present. I think this is the root of our collective anxiety, which is suffering," Daniel said. "It's our inability to face what is. The choice is made. It is what it is and cannot be changed."

If we live with what is, we are facing the reality of what is in the now. We can then make our choices based upon what is. Just one choice, one event, will redirect our path toward another destination. When we choose responsibly, making conscious choices, we become the captain of our journey. If we choose haphazardly, we become victims of the snowball effect, which evolves into an avalanche of compounding effects that bury us alive. We don't know which way is up, and we freeze in our own inability to save ourselves from victimization.

When asked what he used to help himself through his part of the abortion, which was over thirty years ago, Daniel responded, "One of the tools I have learned is being in nature. It reminds me of my significant insignificance. When we are at that young age, we don't understand the power of our words and actions, and the lifelong ramifications they will have."

He still wonders about Lydia. How is she doing with all that occurred, and how the events of 30 years ago have directed her life? He has tried many ways to find her, to no avail. "I still want her to know that I hold her dear in my heart. I wish there was a way to convey this to her."

Daniel never had a strong calling to be a father. It was not in his plans. So, other than him being the last of his family line, he has no regret of not having a family.

Although Daniel did not suffer the guilt, shame, and regret that so many do, he lost the innocence and trust that he and Lydia once shared. These things can never be regained, nor replaced. Once lost, they are forever unattainable.

The regret Daniel did face was the loss of his first love.

Chapter Twelve

The Power of Words

At the time of my abortion, during my near-death experience, one entity stood out among all the rest. I believe this was the soul of my child waiting to welcome me. It is a sense of love beyond anything I can explain. It is ever present. For many years I asked for her forgiveness, and all I ever felt was the pure love and the compassion that I experienced in that moment. Many times since then I have tapped into this realm of nothing but good, where only peace, harmony, and truth abide. It is where all that is to be known, is known.

I have found that all this, and more, is available within my belief. We can integrate this into our life experience now. We do not have to wait until we die. But to attain this we must forgive ourselves and move out of the guilt, shame, and regret. These lower levels of consciousness do not exist in the higher realm. They hold us back from experiencing love, harmony, and balance.

One of the greatest ways we can clear ourselves of the past is by writing a letter. Rose and her sister wrote powerful letters to their children during a ritual to release their collective souls. In fact, communication through writing is a powerful way to deal with any unsolved issue. If we have a challenge with someone, we can write a letter saying anything we desire - anything! Get it all out. Do not hold back.

There is great therapeutic value in writing. Expressing thoughts and defining conflicts on paper allows us to literally see what is on our mind. By editing, clarifying, and sometimes even venting, the writing process often uncovers hidden issues that need attention, or new ideas that warrant exploration. Writing allows us to address our anger and pain, enabling us to work through it. In some cases, our issues include someone else. This can be someone who has hurt us; perhaps it is someone we have hurt. They may be living, or it may be someone who has been dead for many years. The point is to directly address the issues, or people, through writing – let everything out. When we are done with the deep wounded version of our anger, we release the letter by burning it. We let it go.

Then, we write a second letter. This one comes from a more conscious place within. We can keep this letter, if we like, or it can also be burned to signify healing and release of the issues we have been hanging onto. The process may be complete at this stage, but when our issues involve someone else, we may need to take the final step of communicating with that person. The first two letters must be written and destroyed before the third is written and sent. You will find that this third letter will come from the heart, your emotions tempered by thoughtful insight and knowledge.

I have written letters to my mother, father, and my former husband. I have included a letter I wrote to my unborn daughter at the end of this book. What I found interesting was that I believe she understood. My writing not only helped me release much of my grief, but it was a way to send my message to her into the universe.

Chapter Thirteen

Celeste

We go about our lives with particular beliefs that set the tone for how we live. Some thoughts never come to mind, because they are not a part of our every day existence until we are faced with a paradigm shift. Then everything we thought we believed changes, causing us to re-frame our thinking and our actions. Life responds with a new way of living, and everything has shifted because our outlook has changed.

Celeste was forty-two years old, married, and a mother of a ten-year-old daughter. She considered herself to be pro-life, never believing in abortion as the answer to unwanted pregnancy. Celeste and her husband Aaron were very careful about the use of birth control. Other than when they conceived their daughter, the only time they did not use a contraceptive was in the heat of passion one Christmas Eve. The result was an unplanned pregnancy.

Celeste was concerned for her health. Age forty-two was a bit late in life to have another child. Was it safe for her? Was it healthy for the baby? Additionally, Celeste was a child of older parents. Her mother was forty and her father fifty-five when she was born. Celeste simply did not want to be an older mother herself.

"Growing up, my friends had mothers who were hip," Celeste said. "Mine wasn't. My father died when I was in my twenties." She did not want her child to experience the possibility of losing a parent at such a young age.

Celeste and Aaron were also having issues with their marriage at the time, and they didn't want to add a baby into the myriad of concerns. Celeste was considering returning to school to get her master's degree, and being the mother of an infant would put that plan on indefinite hold. They were on the spot. What was the best thing for them to do, considering the circumstances? Abortion was their decision.

Aaron suggested that they conduct a ritual ceremony to release the soul of the baby back to Spirit. They chose, in consciousness, to perform the ritual on the night before the procedure. Just as they sat down, it began to snow. Snow, for Celeste, represents forgiveness. It was a reconciliation of their decision; an acknowledgment that it was the right choice to make.

They burned sage to cleanse the space, played carefully selected music, lit candles, and spoke a beautiful prayer for the soul of the child and for themselves. No one prays like Celeste. When she prays, it is as if her words become sacred objects upon which light is carried to illuminate the way for healing. She prayed that night for the metamorphosis of her child - to be lifted on the wings of angels; for the highest and best of its soul's journey. They also spoke directly to soul of the baby, telling it that bringing it into the world was not the right thing for them. They invited it to move on to someone who would be better able to care for it. Celeste mentioned that her friend, who had been tirelessly trying to conceive a baby, would be a wonderful mother. Celeste had been physically ill during the entire pregnancy. As soon as their ceremony was concluded, the sickness went away.

Celeste and Aaron arrived at the public clinic early the next day. A large fence surrounded the building, with a guard at the gate. Outside the fence were about fifteen anti-abortion protestors carrying signs. One protestor was posted on top of a ladder, peering over the fence and taunting people in the parking lot. Celeste and Aaron sat in a park across the street, carefully observing. They finally passed through the crowd. Celeste said the protestors were intense. She said, "They were judgmental, like they were trying to save you."

The last thing she remembered before entering the building was the woman on the ladder yelling, "You don't have to do this! It's not too late to change your mind!"

Celeste and Aaron were greeted at the door and allowed in. The building was locked down like a prison. "It was like going to an execution," Celeste said. "It made me feel another part of humanity. There was so much compassion. Up to this time I had been feeling holier than thou. We are all just doing the best we can."

Celeste said the room was filled with young women who seemed to have no concept of what they were doing. They were just there to have an abortion, without clarity of thought. Celeste and Aaron sat there for nearly five hours as witnesses for every woman present, sending them a blessing for their best good. At that time, she believes she was given another sign that indicated her decision was the best choice for her. While she was waiting, she shuffled a deck of angel cards, which she utilizes to give her additional guidance. As she shuffled, one fell out that read "Good choice." She believes every step was a confirmation that they were doing the right thing; that they were in alignment with the best choice for the baby and their family.

"This was the cleanest experience I have ever had. There is no guilt," Celeste said. "I had done some personal work years earlier. I got to a state of mind where I knew I was the soul choosing to be in my mother's body. There is no death. The soul remains. I was not killing the soul of my baby, but I was releasing the vessel, so that its soul could move on."

Months later, Celeste and I had the opportunity to participate in a spiritual ceremony, derived from 3000 years of Vedic Indian wisdom. It takes one deeper into a realm of healing that clears the way for a higher consciousness and deeper awareness. During the process, one goes through a clearing where painful memories are revealed so they can be released. This is a method of letting go of known and unknown blocks that hold us back from our higher and greater sense of self. I later spoke with Celeste about her experience that day. Many things arose for her, but not her abortion. She was entirely at peace with it. She has left her abortion behind. She believes she gave the soul of the child back to the spirit realm, where it could move on to a greater existence.

Interestingly enough, just weeks following Celeste's abortion, she received a phone call. Her friend, who for two years had undergone many expensive in-vitro fertilization processes, was calling with the good news that she was finally pregnant. She had twins, a girl, and a boy whom they named Jackson. This is Celeste's favorite name for a boy. A true believer in metaphysics, Celeste considers the possibility that her baby's soul indeed moved on. Her friend never knew about Celeste's abortion, or the favored name.

There are many things we do not understand within the vast realm of possibility. We have limited ability to tap into anything but a small percentage of our brain's capacity. What lies beyond the realm of the known is inestimable. It is infinite in its limitless possibilities. Isn't it amazing to think that what we are not able to do, or provide, is possible in other circumstances where the right timing and perfect conditions make it so? We do not know everything, so why not consider the possibility?

Celeste lives within the healing of what she and Aaron created through their faith in something greater. The ritual to let go of their baby released it into the expanded dimensions for infinite possibilities to occur for its greater good.

Chapter Fourteen

Meditation

Meditation is the most powerful way I have found to come to peace. The word "meditation" is derived from two root words in Latin, *meditari* – to think, to dwell upon; and *mederi* – to heal. In Sanskrit, *medha* – means wisdom. It could be said that to meditate is to go beyond the thinking mind into wisdom, which brings healing. Meditation also comes as a quiet surrender of the self, to open up to what can come forth.

Meditation liberates the energy of the body and mind to a higher expanse of consciousness, resulting in surrender. Through surrender, humility becomes a power that trumps all other forms of human experience. Humility is the realization that we are gifted with the powers of something greater within ourselves. As we let go of the egoic self, we open up to the greater self within. It is a quiet knowing. But we must get ourselves out of our way to be ready to receive our divinity, which is living in the realm of love, peace, truth, harmony, health, with a consciousness of abundance. It is here where we know we are supplied, supported, and surrounded with all we need. It is faith at its best.

Another way to access this place of power is within a physical point in the body. These are the subtle energy fields, referred to as the *chakras*. Between the solar plexus and the heart is the central horizontal earth plane. The vertical plane, starting from the center of the earth to infinity - the Zenith - constitutes our alignment. Where these meet, at the axis point, is the physical point of power within the energy body. The ancient Egyptians used the cross to symbolize this long before Christianity adopted the symbol. It is where the past has no push, the future has no pull, and we are in our most powerful state of being.

Ancient Indian Vedic philosophy teaches us about these subtle energy fields. Yoga is taught using the center field to create balance and equanimity. The chi or qi is the same in Qi Gong, Tai Chi, and in the martial arts. Activating all power from the chi enables one to accomplish great feats of strength and power.

Whenever we are in question of what to do, by going to that center we achieve an awareness of what is needed in the moment. That center of chi, self, Spirit, God, the Universe, whatever you call upon to support you, is ever present in the center of that moment. When this physical axis point is consciously activated, which is at the center of the body temple, the spiritual, mental, and emotional centers come into alignment. Intuition is then set into motion as a mighty power where what we need to know is known in an instant, and our strength is anchored.

This is a form of enlightenment or pure awareness. It is balance, harmony, and order. No matter where we are, or what circumstances we are in when we access this point of power, we then think as our higher nature, speak from our higher nature, and consequently act as our higher nature. We become one with God, the Universe, or what we name the Higher Self. The atmosphere is filled with peace, and nothing but love is present.

Whether we are religious, spiritual, agnostic, or atheist, we can tap into this awareness. We all have the ability to attain this in every moment of every day. It is part of what conscious choice provides us. The more aware we are, the more empowered we become. There are many ways one can meditate. Some access the meditative state while gardening, playing the guitar, walking in nature, or participating in a form of artistic expression. Meditation takes one deeper, where time and space have no significance. It is very personal and intimate. Listening to a guided meditation is a wonderful way to go deeper.

The mediation practice that I use is enhanced by a chakra alignment that I do first. It uses the subtle energy bodies within to empower every aspect of my body, mind, psyche, and the spiritual realm, as it heals and unblocks areas within the mind and body. The chakra system is derived from ancient India. It has been in use for over three thousand years – the longest unbroken religious practice in the world. For millennia, healing practices, including meditation, have been honed, refined, and passed down from generation to generation. The following is derived from one of these meditation practices. I do the Chakra Clearing

Meditation before I meditate. It cleanses me, while putting me into a frame of mind where the meditation is easy to flow into.

Chakra Clearing Meditation

In a quiet, dark setting, perhaps in a room with the drapes drawn, sit in an upright position with your back as straight as possible. If comfortable, sit cross-legged on the floor or on a meditation cushion. Otherwise, sitting on a chair is fine. Sitting with hands on the knees, either close your eyes or use a soft gaze.

The first chakra is located at the perineum. This is the base chakra representing the instinctual subtle body. This is what anchors you to the center of the earth. Visualize the color red. The sound of this chakra is Lang *(Lon)*. While visualizing the color red, place your concentration at the base chakra. Take a deep breath and then chant Lang *(Lon)* as the breath is let out. Repeat this seven times, each time taking a deep breath as you chant the sound. Visualize the color red surrounding your body in an energetic field. Feel yourself deeply grounded to the center of the earth.

The second chakra is located at the level of the sexual organs – this is the creative subtle body. Its color is orange, and its sound is Vang *(Von)*. While visual-izing the color orange, place your concentration at this part of the body. Take a deep breath and chant Vang *(Von)* seven times, each time taking a deep breath as you chant the sound. Visualize the color orange surrounding the body, over the red field, wrapping yourself in its power. Feel the elevation of your creative energy.

The third chakra is located at the solar plexus, about two inches below the belly button. This subtle energy is the center of the body. This is where you get your "gut reactions." Its color is yellow, and its sound is Rang *(Ron)*. While visualizing the color yellow, concentrate on the center of your body. Take a deep breath and chant Rang *(Ron)* seven times, each time taking a deep breath as you chant. Visualize the color yellow wrapping around the color orange, which is wrapped around the red. Feel the energy of your centeredness surrounding you.

The fourth chakra is located at the heart. This is the subtle energy of the heart, where you feel deeply. Its color is green, and its sound is Yang *(Yon)*. While visualizing the color green, take a deep breath, concentrating on your heart center, and chant Yang *(Yon)* seven times, each time taking a deep breath as you chant. Visualize the color green wrapping around the color yellow, which is around the orange, which is around the red. You are now surrounded by the energy of your heart.

The fifth chakra is located at the throat. This is the subtle energy of the voice, the ability to be heard. Its color is dark blue, and its sound is Hang *(Hon)*. While visualizing the color dark blue, place your concentration at the level of the throat, take a deep breath and chant Hang *(Hon)* seven times, each time taking a deep breath as you chant. Visualize the color dark blue surrounding the color green, which is around the yellow, orange, and red. You are now surrounded by the power of your every word.

The sixth chakra is located at the third eye – just above and between the eyebrows. This is the subtle energy of intuition, the still small voice within. Its color is violet, and its sound is Aum *(Aw-oom)*. While visualizing the color violet, place your concentration at the level of the third eye, take a deep breath and chant

Aum (*Aw-oom*) seven times, each time taking a deep breath as you chant. Visualize the color violet as it wraps around your body surrounding the dark blue, green, yellow, orange, and red. You are now surrounded by the power of your intuition, the still, small voice within.

The seventh and final chakra is at the crown, located at the top of your head. This is the subtle body of the God essence. It is your connection to the Infinite. Its color is white, and its sound is Om. While visualizing the color white, place your concentration at the crown. Take a deep breath and chant Om seven times, each time taking a deep breath as you chant. Visualize the color white wrapping your body over the violet, dark blue, green, yellow, orange, and red. You are now surrounded by your divinity with all the layers of yourself underneath each other, empowered to be your best self. You are anchored to the earth on the horizontal plane and connected to the Divine at the same time on the vertical plane. You are fully aligned. Your greatest energy is at the center between solar plexus and the heart. This is your place of power.

Daily meditation helps to maintain alignment with

your higher nature. It empowers every level of your subtle body to be its strongest, as it raises every part of your being to its highest vibratory level. As you are visualizing the colors, see them becoming bright and vibrant to a brilliance that fills that area of your body and consequently surrounds you in the power of that energetic field.

You may find that you are releasing blocks, feeling better, are more energized, and radiate a field of energy throughout your day that is noticeable to others. You may find that you heal yourself from the power that lies within. Not only are the subtle energies physical fields, but they are also emotional, mental, and spiritual fields as well. When all of these are powered up, you feel your best. You also draw others to you at every level, for they are attracted to your radiance.

Following the Chakra Clearing, I sit in silent meditation. I open up to what the silence allows. When thoughts come to mind, I allow them to float by like a leaf on a river. I stay in the silence until I sense that I am finished. Sometimes this is fifteen minutes, and other times it is two hours. I typically do this in the middle of the night, when there is nothing to distract me.

Meditation creates a more peaceful way of living. When confronted with the common irritants that arise each day, the practice of meditation allows us to let the challenge go by, just like the leaf on the surface of the river. It helps to clear the mind of unnecessary chatter, and leads to healing.

Chapter Fifteen

Evelyn

At the age of ninety, Evelyn was an incredible woman. She was a widow, having been married for fifty-six years. She met her husband after World War II. They had four children, nine grandchildren, and three great-grandchildren.

Shortly before she died, Evelyn revealed to her favorite granddaughter, Sophie, a secret about a lost love prior to meeting Sophie's grandfather. Evelyn was studying to become a nurse in San Diego at the beginning of the war. She occasionally volunteered for the Red Cross when they needed extra help. One of the patients she cared for was Joseph, a young sailor who was injured during basic training.

Evelyn fell in love with the handsome dark-haired boy, whom she lovingly called Joey. Evelyn's beauty, strength of character, and warm heart enchanted him. They were inseparable, spending many evenings walking on the beach. Their time together passed by too quickly, however, for Joey was soon called up for duty overseas. A few nights before he left, Joey proposed marriage. Evelyn couldn't say yes fast enough. Neither of them slept that night. They remained entangled in love's embrace, as if to embody the moment for memory's sake.

Evelyn was nineteen; Joey was twenty-two. They made plans to marry immediately when he returned home from duty. A few weeks later, she discovered she was pregnant. It would be fine. She would go ahead and have the baby. Everyone would understand, with the war and all. She wrote Joey a letter to tell him about the baby. On her way to the mailbox, two young sailors, who were friends of Joey, met her on the porch. They regretfully gave her the news of Joey's death, which occurred during an air raid. He never knew what hit him.

Two of Evelyn's girlfriends knew about the pregnancy. So filled with grief beyond comprehension,

Evelyn didn't know what to do next. How would she be able to raise a baby by herself? She would be shunned by the community. She was not yet a nurse, and would be unable to finish her schooling for several years. She had no income to speak of. Joey just started to send her a portion of his pay to build a nest egg for their life together. Joey's family was not the type to help her out. Her family, who lived in Iowa, knew very little of her relationship with the young man. As far as her parents knew, Evelyn dated around and was not steady with anyone.

She regretfully decided to have an abortion. Her friends drove her to Tijuana, where they knew of a woman who could take care of Evelyn's problem. They stayed there for a few days following the abortion to give Evelyn a little time to recover before returning to school. Evelyn eventually became a nurse, and she began to pick up the pieces, but it took a couple of years before she worked through the loss of both Joey and her baby. Years later, she met and married Sophie's grandfather.

Evelyn never spoke of Joey or her abortion, leaving a scar that remained unhealed. Harboring this secret until she was close to death, Evelyn finally revealed it to Sophie, the first time she had spoken of this to anyone. It had been over sixty years since the death of Joey, and also the death of her first child.

When she told Sophie, tears streamed down the wrinkles of her sweet face. Sophie cried along with her, allowing her grandmother to open up to the flood of tears. They shared the grief that plagued her for decades. For Evelyn, it was as if it had just happened yesterday. The grief remained fresh. She kept it alive, because she bottled it up and never let it go.

Evelyn finally felt free of her dark secret; liberated from the prison she kept herself in for over half a century. Simply by speaking a sentence or two of the truth, she transcended all suffering instantly. We often hang onto unnecessary self-imposed shame, considering ourselves less than worthy, as if we are paying some sort of penance for our mistakes and sins. The word 'sin' means without. Somehow we think that by doing without, we are paid back through our grievances. Martyrdom is not a badge of honor. It is a silent form of self-flagellation that leaves scars on the psyche. No good ever comes from shame or guilt. They only perpetuate more of the same. We must raise ourselves out of this dark suffering.

We must be like the trapeze artist who lets go of the bar on faith. As she releases the bar, she turns in mid air, reaching out for the hands that she trusts are reaching for her. Grasping firmly to what she is seeking, she moves forward to a new destination. Willingness to let go of the past, and trusting the firm hands of the future to catch us, is a quantum leap of faith. Faith is living within a framework of high consciousness and trusting that what we seek is also seeking us. When we let go of our encumbrances and face a new direction, we can then move on.

Evelyn lived a good life. By telling her story to Sophie, she "let go of the bar." She died knowing that she honored not only her husband and family, but also Joey and their child. Through one short conversation, she brought instantaneous healing to a deep wound of over sixty years.

All it takes is reaching out to one friend, one confidant, to courageously open up the heart.

Chapter Sixteen

Give the Children a Voice

The children we have left behind cannot speak for themselves. Yet, through our memory they remain, lingering in our every waking moment. Once touched by someone's life, they never leave us. Our lives are never the same. The soul of the child becomes a part of the design of our patchwork quilt. However, the voice of the children we have left behind can now be heard as we give life to the stories we previously denied.

When we remember and honor the children we chose to release, we give them a voice. If we allow them to be a part of our experience, we bring life to what was once buried. By speaking of them, even to one other person, we free them from the prison in which we hold them hostage. We shed light upon the darkest corners of what we have hidden.

The children are not silent. They speak in a language that is not verbal, yet we converse with them through our dreams. Our innermost secrets arise seemingly out of nowhere when we commune with the faceless spirits of our past.

The mystical essence of our children is the morning dew upon the open petals of summer flowers. It is the newness in every aspect of nature - their iridescence reflects the new dawn, leaving an invisible layer, ever penetrating our very being. We breathe their very breath. They have touched us in such a way that we peer at the world through the eyes of the soul that they left behind. Our hearts beat a bit stronger, supported by the rhythm of their vibration. Never gone and ever present, they remain interlaced within our being. The fabric of their soul is intertwined with our life experience, colored with threads that weave within our thoughts, words, and deeds.

Humility is but one of the gifts they have left behind. Compassion and empathy are additions to our experience. Their small voices speak in gentle tones, as a whisper of memory's touch upon our hearts. The gentle breeze carries their spirit upon the wisp of the wind. Sunrays penetrate the generosity of their souls' strength. Waves wash upon the beach, lapping the cadence of their heartbeat. Wings of eagles carry their message to heights above the clouds, never to be forgotten. Nature's call to the infinite expansive realm is their voice speaking with the silent strength of everlasting expansion.

Every infant we encounter holds the essence of our child. Their laughter is the harmonic blend of the soul of every baby, reverberating pure joy. The tears they shed are the collective hearts of the life-giving force. They contain elements of the world's woes and heart-break. When one baby cries, the universe listens with compassion. Gentle tenderness is a reflection of the spirit that exudes an ease and grace within the funda-mental nature of the child. Nothing is more powerful. Nothing holds the heart like a child. They are the collective spirit of all who have never been.

Their souls are everywhere. A part of us, they are what feed our desires to be better people. Through our every action we express the essence of our child. We experience their soul in the stars that shine. We see their reflection in the snowflake's individual pattern, which collected together blanket the mountain's wintery expression. The newness of spring, as the first crocus peering through the snow, is the gentle perseverance of the soul breaking through every barrier. The soul remains the quintessential core of life.

Their infinite souls triumphantly move with us, for the soul is ever present in its ubiquitous journey. Life continues. We are enhanced by the tiny beings that are ever a part of our lives. We honor them, opening our hearts to the multifaceted, crystal clarity of the soul that connects us to the golden thread of truth, entwining us in the spiritual realm. It is here where we join our children in the community of the spirit. We connect in our dreams, our mediations, and in our prayers.

With gratitude, we thank the children for what they have taught us. Never will we be the same. Ever changed, we now live with the conscious awareness that they are a part of our upward spiral journey as we expand into greater dimensions.

We bless their souls' journey and send them great love. Giving them a voice, we remember who they are and what they mean to us. We shed a tear, like the crystal reflection of their quintessence. The life force of the world remains as the carrier of the soul of our child, living out loud, giving our children a voice.

Chapter Seventeen

Mystic Atonement

I cannot emphasize enough the importance of literally turning thoughts into words, and words into action. Writing our thoughts into a journal or diary allows us to organize the conglomeration of emotions that float in our minds. It is similar to listening to your own recorded voice – what you hear in your head is very different than what you hear with your ears. I emphasize what I've said before - putting our thoughts on paper enables us to literally see into our minds. Something that might make perfect sense in the quiet solitude of your mind may be entirely absurd when you read it aloud. Conversely, something insignificant or confusing may suddenly make perfect sense when you see it on paper.

Writing about the grief, anger, or shame that we feel about the abortion experience allows us to face our demons and triumph over them. For example, writing this book has been tremendously cathartic for me. For two years, I have thought, dreamed, written, and read about grief and forgiveness. It has been a part of every day. I took this book, in thought, to Greece, while I sat on the ruins of Delphi. It has traveled with me to the shores of Kauai, and to the Lake of the Ozarks. Even in Las Vegas, I have walked the streets of never-ending electric energy; I left my thoughts behind as I took my steps along the boulevard.

I now share what I have learned with the hope of helping others who are struggling with their abortion. Any form of artistic expression is an extension of our innermost thoughts. To leave something behind, in form, is a tribute to those from our past. Dedicating your life's calling to your unborn child is an amazing way to pay tribute to her or his memory. If you have a personal altar where sacred objects are kept, perhaps something that represents the essence of your child could be placed there to be remembered and honored daily.

Growing a garden, planting a tree or a rose bush - giving back to nature is a way to remember. The catharsis of painting a picture, writing a poem or book, or journal gives back, simply because you are clearing your heart and mind of memories that have blocked your freedom of expression. Spending time in nature, witnessing the world with new eyes is renewing. Every action that is life-giving and creative generates a spark of light, reconciling anything that was once regretful.

Our intentions and actions to help a child, the elderly, or to raise an animal with grace all gives back to the universe. If we create from heart, with gratitude and from a deep and abiding joy, we expand what once was diminished. The sacred is created out of what was once profane. Beauty is extended from what was thought of as dark and lifeless. Freedom and liberation comes from what we have released into the ether.

So, what have I gained by going back into the memories of my abortion? I have gained empathy for all those who feel guilt and shame for something that caused themselves or others pain. I have honored my feelings as I opened up to deep grief, allowing it to surface and thus freeing myself. I have found the formula to help myself heal my past wounds. As a result, I now have beautiful memories that I had once blocked. They now fill the empty spaces of the jigsaw puzzle of my life. I live in forgiveness and gratitude. As I forgive, I let go and release my hold on what no longer serves me.

Living in gratitude, in thanksgiving for all that I experience, I now allow life to bring me more of what I am grateful for, thus living in an upward spiral of growth and change. Having the opportunity to visit the next dimension, I have tapped into a deeper perspective of what life offers. It is infinite in its possibilities and grand beyond description.

I have a sweet and tender relationship with the spirit of my daughter, for I believe that she is with me as a loving soul supporting me in this life's journey. I came back to be a healer/teacher. I was given the choice. I returned to be a unique expression of my spiritual essence as I help others seek their greatness.

The journey continues. It never ends. What I continue to glean from this adventure of life and its multi-dimensional levels of existence is eternal. The infinite awareness is available in each and every moment. It is accessed through choice. By surrendering to the higher nature within, we shift through the illusion of the turbulent storm and enter into the eye, where there is peace, joy, and wonderment of the next adventure in our journey.

All this, and more, I give to you.

Chapter Eighteen

A Letter to my Daughter

Dear Lanie,

I have given you the name of my mother, which was Elizabeth Elaine. Both names were originally Greek and later, Irish. Elizabeth means, "My God is my oath." Elaine - "Light, torch, and bright." I interpret the combination to mean, "I am the promise of Divine Illumination." Both you and my mother have been a beacon that illuminated my direction. In healing the past, the ship upon which I sail is the present leading to the destinations of my intended future.

Your grandmother, had you known her, was a beautiful dark-Irish woman with auburn hair and hazel-green eyes. In her prime, she was proud, intelligent, elegant, and stunningly beautiful. In my most fond memory of her I remember her laughing until she lit up the room. This was rare. She had a dark energy. Growing up with my mother was an invitation for me to counteract that low vibration. So, in my writing I heal the memories of the past. This brings me to the center of my being, where I can live in forgiveness of her and for myself. I am then free to set sail upon clear waters.

I envision you as a vibrant, creative child who has the same sense of beauty as your grandmother. I see you living from the reality of joy and creative expression like your grandmother did when she was at her best. I imagine you to be intelligent and wise beyond your years. You have what some know as being an old soul. You would love to learn. It would come easily to you. Everywhere you would go – life would be an adventure, and it would show up in miraculous ways.

Compassion of the heart would have been your hallmark. You would have seen the universe through the lives of others with whom you are in company. You would have become a traveler, absorbing the atmosphere of your surroundings, taking with you every minute detail. It would have become a part of your being. Your charismatic nature would have invited the stranger into your circle, embracing life and reflecting the joy that you personified. Touched and changed, each would have been transformed as you expanded through the exchange of souls. Peace and love would have resided at the center of you. You simply would have been blessed every-where you went as you radiated the essence of God to everyone you encountered.

I have come to you, in the form of writing, to let you know how very much you are loved by me. At the time I let you go, I thought it was safer for me to try to forget you. It was so difficult for me to admit that I had to release you. Now, as I honestly reflect my fears and failures, as well as my triumphs and achievements, I come to you with a transparent heart. Forgiveness and gratitude are the filters through which I clear the past. What results is the peace and harmony that I know is my birthright. It is time for me to open to the gifts of what this experience of abortion brings.

I know that, at the deepest level, you are aware of why I released you from my body before you could be my daughter. Even at the time, I sensed that I had your permission to allow me to let you go. It was the innate elegance of you that I felt as a great love radiating beyond the pain of the decision to have the abortion.

It was a decision that I had to make. No other choice was evident. The grief of the loss of you still resides deep within. This is why I am writing – to convey to you what I have done to come full circle in what has been my journey of atonement.

The journey I have chosen – that of embracing all that has occurred - rides upon the mystical ship that supports my healing. The following is my voyage as I am returning, full circle, to myself again.

I never heard you cry. I have spent decades wondering what it would have been like to hold you in my arms - to rock you into a tender sleep. I never got to gently bathe you as an infant. There was no sweet scent of you as a baby – unlike any other scent. I missed the opportunity to dress you in beautiful dresses, and also in jeans and little sweaters along with tiny tennis shoes. I never got a chance to take care of you when you had to stay home sick from school - to bring you breakfast in bed, to pamper and care for you until you felt well again. I never had the opportunity to attend your school play, or to watch you in your high school tennis matches. I did not hear about the sweetness of your first kiss. No graduation. No wedding. No grandchildren. No mother-daughter moments.

The only time I was a mother of any kind was during the eight weeks that you were in my body. In order to survive the decision that I made to let you go, I kept myself emotionally devoid so I could follow through with what I knew I had to do. I didn't even let you know that I loved you when you and

I were together. I am so sorry that I was not present enough to let you know that you mattered.

I can tell you now that your presence in my life does matter to me. It has affected my journey ever since that day. No one has had the profound impact upon my life as you have. I thank you deeply for your presence – for I continue to feel it with me each and every day.

I think it is one reason, now, why I am so touched by the beauty of nature. It is part of my atonement, as I recognize the preciousness of all life. I had shut down for quite a while, but life just kept showing up to meet me with invitations to join with it again.

I did what was necessary to save my own life. Now, I formally ask for your forgiveness as I work through releasing myself from these shackles that have silently held me back. They are the worst of prisons – shame, doubt, and guilt. They are what held me back from anything that would propel me to my greatness, thus creating in me the belief that I do not deserve it. I felt I had no choice but to let you go. But how could I move forward if I did not allow you to come into this world as my daughter?

I am grateful to you for coming to me as an advanced being, and for choosing to come to me in the way that you did. I cannot help but believe that you knew, in advance, your purpose for being in my life.

I now choose a conscious life, a purposeful life; because I was not as conscious at the time we were together during those eight short weeks. Consequently, I have made choices because of my experience of you, not in spite of it. It was that pivotal point when I changed my course to a greater destination beyond my cognition.

From what I have experienced since that time, which seems so long ago, I now know that love transcends all barriers. I know that I have many angels and guides that surround me. Perhaps I am, in essence, one of those for you, as you are for me. Through my experience in the multi-dimensional levels of life, I know the veil is thin between the numerous levels of consciousness. Love expands beyond time and space. So, I send you my love from the depths of my being. It kisses you on the cheek with tenderness, transcending all physical barriers.

There will be a day when we will meet. I will know that it is you who stands before me, for our souls know no separation. Until then, on behalf of you, I send my love to all beings as I see the God in them. I feel the essence of all children as if they were my own. I gaze into the eyes of every human; into *windows of the soul, knowing that therein is the essence of God beneath the shell of the body's façade.*

When I am filled with the peace of nature as it aligns with me, my body is straightened as I stand grounded in the heart of God. I am then lifted into the ether of the vibration most high to its zenith. I radiate the light of God, and this is where you and I meet with all beings - where we meld together in oneness. The horizontal earthly realm, intersected by the vertical alignment of the spiritual, creates the axis point - the center of all power. It is here, in the center of being, where we have never experienced separation and never shall.

I thank you for what you continue to teach me. You have become me, as I have lived through what I know your spirit to be. In the oneness of our being, I am you, as well. From the depths of my heart, I send you my love each and every day, knowing that we are not without the other. I pass on to you what my father said to me just before he died . . . You are my precious, darling little girl!

~ Your Mother

Acknowledgments

Plotting the course of this book has been a journey I could not have sailed without the support of many. First and foremost, I am thankful to my beloved husband and editor, Kevin Cahill. Without his knowledge of the written word and his wisdom of the heart, this work would not have been finished for many years. His generous nature and patience allowed me everything I needed to dedicate my time and energies to my writing. I am so very grateful.

Additionally, I am very thankful to Sadie Tourtillott for her loving nature, time and expertise. Every week, for months, she read the chapters with me, editing for content. She kept me on track, making sure that my writing was authentic, honorable, and true to the spirit of the book.

The book would not have been complete without the individuals who shared their stories. I kept their anonymity sacred. Without them, I would not have been able to generate a work of heart, reaching out to many whose own story is yet to be revealed. Each of these courageous people eagerly came forth with an honest account of their experience and an authentic willingness to share both their pain and healing.

There are dozens of people I have counseled with and confided in about the topic. Everyone was completely supportive. I received nothing negative from anyone. Most of them encouraged me to write this, speaking to its great need. Lastly, I am grateful for Homer's guidance, for without it, I would not have found the formula for healing, which led to this book.

I am simply grateful for the opportunity to bring this work of heart forward to reveal healing of an age old elephant in the room.

Selected Reading

Beckwith, Michael Bernard. *Spiritual Liberation – Fulfilling Your Soul's Potential*. New York: Atria Books, 2008.

_____ *The Answer is You*. Los Angeles: Agape Media International, 2009.

Braden, Gregg. *The Divine Matrix - Bridging Time, Space, Miracles, and Belief*. Carlsbad, CA: Hay House, 2007.

_____ *Secrets of the Lost Mode of Prayer*. Carlsbad, CA: Hay House, 2006.

Chopra, Deepak. *The Seven Spiritual Laws of Success – A Practical Guide to the Fulfillment of Your Dreams*. Novato, CA: New World Library, 1994.

Dispenza, Joe. *Evolve your Brain*. Deerfield Beach, FL: Health Communications, 2007.

Dyer, Wayne W. *There's a Spiritual Solution to Every Problem*. New York: HarperCollins Publishers, 2001.

_____ *The Power of Intention – Learning to Co-create Your World Your Way*. Carlsbad, CA: Hay House, 2004.

_____ *Change Your Thoughts – Change Your Life – Living the Wisdom of the Tao*. Carlsbad, CA: Hay House, 2007.

Goldsmith, Joel S. *The Art of Spiritual Healing*. New York: HarperCollins Publishers, 1992.

Hawkins, David R. *Power vs. Force*. Carlsbad, CA: Hay House, 2002.

Hay, Louise L. *The Power is Within You*. Carson, CA: Hay House, 1991.

His Holiness the Dalai Lama. *An Open Heart – Practicing Compassion in Everyday Life*. Boston: Little Brown and Company, 2001.

His Holiness the Dalai Lama; Victor Chan. *The Wisdom of Forgiveness – Intimate Conversations and Journeys*. New York: Riverhead Books, 2004.

Holliwell, Raymond. *Working With the Law*. Scottsdale, AZ: LifeSuccess Productions, 2007.

Holmes, Ernest. *The Science of Mind – A Philosophy, A Faith, A Way of Life*. New York: Jeremy P. Tarcher/Penguin, 1998.

_____ *Love & Law – the Unpublished Teachings*. New York: Jeremy P. Tarcher/Penguin, 2001.

_____ *Words That Heal Today*. Deerfield Beach, FL: Health Communications, 1999.

Kubler-Ross, Elisabeth. *On Death and Dying*. New York: Macmillan Publishing Company, 1974

Levine, Stephen. *Guided Meditations, Explorations and Healings*. New York: Anchor Books, 1991.

Levine, Stephen and Ondrea. *Unattended Sorrow – Recovering from Loss and Reviving the Heart*. Emmaus, PA: Rodale, 2005.

Lipton, Bruce H. *The Biology of Belief – Unleashing the Power of Consciousness, Matter & Miracles*. Carlsbad, CA: Hay House, 2008.

Nerburn, Kent. *Simple Truths*. Novato, CA: New World Library, 1996.

Orloff, Judith. *Guide to Intuitive Healing – 5 Steps to Physical, Emotional, and Sexual Wellness.* New York: Three Rivers Press, 2000.

_____ *Emotional Freedom – Liberate Yourself from Negative Emotions and Transform Your Life.* New York: Harmony Books, 2009.

Rosenthal, Sheri; Reeve, Susyn. *With Forgiveness – Are You Ready?* Ashland, OR: Pass Along Concepts, 2006.

Ruiz, Don Miguel. *The Four Agreements.* San Rafael, CA: Amber-Allen Publishing, 1997.

Stone, Tom. *The Power of How – Simple Techniques to Vaporize Your Ego and Your Pain–body.* Carlsbad, CA: Great Life Technologies, 2008.

Tipping, Colin C. *Radical Forgiveness.* Marietta, GA: Global Thirteen Publications, 2007.

_____ *The Way of Mastery.* Ashland, OR: Shanti Christo Foundation, 2009.

_____ *The Prosperity Bible.* New York: Jeremy P. Tarcher/Penguin, 2007.

Tolle, Eckhart. *The Power of Now.* Novato, CA: New World Library, 2004.

_____ *A New Earth.* New York: Plume, 2005.

Walsch, Neale Donald. *Home with God – In a Life That Never Ends.* New York: Atria Books, 2006.

Yogananda, Paramahansa. *The Second Coming of Christ – The Resurrection of the Christ Within You.* Los Angeles: Self-Realization Fellowship, 2007.